brilliant

PR

PR

Create a PR sensation,
whatever your budget,
whatever your business

Cathy Bussey

Prentice Hall
is an imprint of

Harlow, England • London • New York • Boston • San Francisco • Toronto • Sydney • Singapore • Hong Kong
Tokyo • Seoul • Taipei • New Delhi • Cape Town • Madrid • Mexico City • Amsterdam • Munich • Paris • Milan

PEARSON EDUCATION LIMITED

Edinburgh Gate
Harlow CM20 2JE
Tel: +44 (0)1279 623623
Fax: +44 (0)1279 431059
Website: www.pearsoned.co.uk

First published in Great Britain in 2011

ISBN: 978-0-273-74658-4

British Library Cataloguing-in-Publication Data
A catalogue record for this book is available from the British Library

Library of Congress Cataloging-in-Publication Data
Bussey, Cathy.
  Brilliant PR : create a PR sensation, whatever your budget, whatever your
business / Cathy Bussey.
    p. cm.
  Includes bibliographical references and index.
  ISBN 978-0-273-74658-4 (pbk.)
  1. Public relations. I. Title.
  HM1221.B88 2011
  659.2--dc22
                              2011007574

ARP Impression 98

Typeset in 10/14pt Plantin by 30
Printed in Great Britain by Clays Ltd, St Ives plc

For my brilliant husband, Noel

Contents

About the author

Cathy Bussey is deputy editor at PR industry 'bible' *PRWeek*. She has worked as a journalist for eight years at daily and weekly newspapers and magazines and also spent time working as a communications officer for an NHS trust.

Acknowledgements

First and foremost, I would like to thank my incredible agent, Isabel Atherton at Creative Authors, for her belief, drive, encouragement and enthusiasm. She is a brilliant inspiration.

Thank you to everyone who has helped me with my research for this book. In particular I would like to thank Laura Downton at Carswell Gould, Matt Cornish the editor extraordinaire, Sally Churchward, fabulous features writer and ethical queen, Caz Nicklin at Cyclechic, Cate Sevilla at Bitchbuzz.com and founder of the Oh My Blog workshops, Lucy Frankel at Vegaware, Adrienne Cohen for putting me in touch with Lucy, Catherine Birch at Silver Birch Design and the Tribe, and Gemma Massey at Gemma Massey PR.

Thank you to Sam Jackson and Rachel Hayter at Pearson for allowing me to write this hopefully brilliant book.

I must also thank the team at *PRWeek*, my colleagues for the last two years, and to the UK PR industry whose brains I have most definitely picked!

And finally thank you to my mum and dad, Fran and Dave Wallace, because they are both truly brilliant.

Introduction

We are entering the age of the small business. Technology has empowered the individual in ways undreamed of just 20 years ago. Tales of 'bedroom businesses' and successful enterprises started up using just a laptop and an idea abound.

I have spent my career working within the media, firstly at newspapers and magazines, and latterly writing about the PR industry at trade bible *PRWeek*. I have witnessed the power of PR to change a company's fortunes, and the power of bad PR to send those fortunes nosediving.

If anything the recession has made PR more vital than ever. A good reputation is simply essential for a business to thrive. Consumers demand transparency and openness and PR is uniquely placed to help a business offer this. Unlike advertising, PR does not require an investment to generate results.

And then we have the digital revolution, the growth of social media and networking sites like Facebook and Twitter, and the rise of the conversation. The PR industry and the media have both had to adapt, because the public is no longer simply sitting and passively listening to the messages brands and businesses are trying to get to them through advertising and PR. The public is talking back and now it is the media and the business world that must sit up and listen.

But whilst considering all of these factors it did occur to me that the small business, the start-up and the entrepreneur may be rich in ideas but not necessarily in cash. All available funds go into the creation of their enterprise. There is no money left for marketing. They can't afford to pay someone to do their PR for them.

One of the great things about PR is that it can be learned, and anybody can do it. As a journalist with a wealth of experience dealing with PR professionals, and with many contacts within the media who also have this wealth of experience, why should I and we not be sharing this information with the people who really need it?

Brilliant PR will help you manage your own PR and save you money by sharing with you tricks of the trade and secrets that the PR industry would prefer you did not know. Whether you are starting a business, own a business already or you have just started in a PR or marketing role and want to get some background knowledge, *Brilliant PR* has been written to demystify PR and help you understand how to use it to your advantage.

My aim is to teach you *how* to present yourself and your business, product or your client to the public – mainly via the media – in a positive manner to improve your reputation, your business or your client's reputation, and ultimately help make you more money. The book will look at all the basic skills required to carry out a PR strategy, for yourself and your business, or for a product or client that you are representing. It will look at how to create a brand proposition, deal with the media and build good relationships, examine the elements involved in a PR campaign, talk you step-by-step through pitching a story to a media outlet, and help you manage any crises or problems you may encounter. It will use real-life examples to demonstrate what makes 'good' PR – and what makes 'bad' PR.

Whether you are one of the bedroom entrepreneurs to which I have referred above, with a brand spanking new business but no PR budget, or new to marketing and PR and want to know all the trade secrets, without paying a professional to help you, this book will give you all the information you need to put together and carry out a PR strategy. Anyone who needs lessons from the PR experts, but does not have the budget to recruit a company, can learn what they need to know from this book.

CHAPTER 1

What is PR?

Have you had 'that moment' yet? The moment when you open a newspaper, magazine or your trade publication only to see a direct business rival grinning out at you?

Whether you bake the most delicious cupcakes in the world and are gnashing your teeth at the ubiquity of a rival baker, or your latest product launch has been upstaged by a rival having a party for *their* product launch on the diary page of your trade publication, the frustration is the same. Why are they in the papers – and why aren't you?

It's no coincidence. In the same way that we see the same celebrities on the cover of tabloid newspapers, the reason is that, behind the scenes, teams of people are working night and day to get these people, companies and organisations in the media spotlight.

Not only that, but these teams are also working to get the right stories about their clients in the media. It's no use having a story about your client in the papers if the story is a negative one. Companies and celebrities have strategic teams working for them devising ways to get their names in the papers, in the right context, with the right messages.

Welcome to the world of PR. Or, if you prefer, 'spin'.

definition

'PR'

PR, or public relations to give it its full name, is the art of presenting a company (or person) to the public, usually via the media, ideally in a positive manner that improves the reputation of that company (or person) and subsequently impacts positively on that company's sales/uptake of that company's services/the company or individual's overall reputation.

The above definition is not a dictionary definition and seasoned professionals will argue that PR should not, in fact, be called PR at all but 'communications' or 'comms' or 'strategic all-encompassing reputation management'. For the purposes of this book I'm going stick to the brilliant definition and leave the PR professionals to squabble over what PR is or is not.

Why PR?

PR will not offer you an immediate return on your investment. And, as we will discuss below, there are no guarantees. You may have to put a lot of time and effort into putting together your PR strategy, and at some point you may ask yourself 'why am I doing this?' At times like this it is worth remembering a good PR strategy can help or even achieve all of these things:

- Establish you as an expert in your field.
- Drive sales.
- Draw traffic to your website.
- Raise awareness about who you are and what you do.
- Build and maintain a positive reputation for yourself.

In short, PR can really add fuel to your business, your product or your client and be the difference between a good, well-run business that is struggling, and a good, well-run business that is making huge profits.

 example

Caz Nicklin runs Cyclechic.co.uk, a website selling fashionable cycling accessories:

'I have always read the Sunday papers and love the supplements, so I had a good knowledge of the sort of subjects they liked and what made a good feature. I used this knowledge to contact about five journalists initially, to announce the launch of Cyclechic. My big break was *TimeOut*, as we got a full-page feature on our Bern helmets in the Consume section. The Consume editor was then writing a piece for the *Observer* magazine and she listed us as a trend to watch out for that autumn. That had a snowball effect and we were subsequently featured in *Vogue*, The *Daily Telegraph*, *The Week* and *Red* magazine in the space of three months.'

Cyclechic is now a successful UK business that has attracted investment, and Caz recently launched in the US. There is no doubt that the site has tapped into a demand from predominantly female consumers for pretty, elegant cycling accessories, and furthermore that cycling has really begun to boom in recent years. But there are many cycling-related businesses out there that do not enjoy the same profile as Cyclechic and have not been able to expand internationally. Caz's clever use of PR has helped her business really flourish.

She is still working hard to make sure her business remains in the public eye and recently had a profile in the Entrepreneurs section of the *London Evening Standard*.

PR is not rocket science. As Caz Nicklin demonstrates, PR is a skill that can be learned and it involves a good deal of good, old-fashioned common sense. Yes, a creative mind helps and yes, those who are the most successful at PR do tend to be of a certain personality type – outgoing, persuasive and very charming. But the great thing about PR (or the bad thing, for the PR industry) is that anyone can learn the PR basics, master and perfect them.

What PR involves

There are various elements that make up the wonderful world of public relations.

Media relations

Media relations is a crucial element of PR and involves developing relationships with journalists in order to better inform them about you and your product. If a journalist does not know about you, how can they write about you? Media relations can sometimes seem like bribery – you give a journalist a nice treat, such as taking them to lunch, and the journalist will write nice things about you.

But this is a crude and unrealistic way to look at the relationship between PR professionals and their media contacts. You, as the PR professional in question here, must always remember you cannot buy coverage – you cannot buy a journalist. All you can hope for is to keep relations between yourself and journalists as favourable as possible. And the journalist, if they are fair and decent, will hopefully remember that whilst they are under no obligation to do so, if they want a quote from someone like you and have ten people they could call, as you made the effort to build relations with them (by taking them to lunch perhaps) they will call you and not your direct rival.

 **tip**

Journalists have a fairly bad name – they are regularly cited up there with estate agents and lawyers as the professionals the public dislikes and distrusts the most. Why should you bother building up relationships with them? Money might be tight, why waste it taking a journalist out or offering them access to your products, client or services? Always remember that journalists are representatives of the public. You can talk to, or give a free sample to, one person, and if you are lucky they might tell a few people about you. But if you talk to a journalist or give them a free sample, they may talk to potentially hundreds, thousands or even millions of people about you.

The media has changed dramatically in recent years, even since I began working as a reporter on a local paper just seven years ago. The internet, the economy, the constant advances in technology, the consistent desire from consumers for more, better, faster, cheaper, means the media is unrecognisable from what it was 20 years ago. Once upon a time journalists knew everyone in their local communities or the sectors about which they wrote, and would spend days investigating leads to craft their stories. Now newsrooms are emptier, jobs are fewer, and those journalists who survive are increasingly chained to their desks breaking news online that will be 'old news' in five minutes time. The upshot of these changes, which we will look at in more detail throughout this book, is that journalists now need PR more than ever before. It is a sad time for the industry – but a wonderful opportunity for PR and, therefore, for you.

Campaigns

A PR campaign is a series of activities that are planned in advance and put together in such a way as to maximise the opportunities for positive media coverage. Campaigns can include activities such as launches and events, targeting media, promotions and other initiatives, and in the case of large brands, often tie in with a wider marketing or advertising campaign. Campaigns are characterised by robust planning to make the most of opportunities. For example, if you were a bike retailer or ran a cycling business like Cyclechic in the example earlier, you might plan a campaign around National Bike Week, involving an open event at your store, a new product launch and a celebrity endorsement. Because of the timing and the fact that the media would be already interested in cycling, it is likely you would get featured somewhere and receive attention that you normally otherwise would not.

Online presence and social networking

You absolutely have to have a website these days – there is just no getting around it. But if you limit your online presence to just a website, you are missing out. Social media is the new big thing in the world of media and PR and the successful businesses are those with a website, a Facebook page, a Twitter feed, content appearing on YouTube, and so on. Get these channels right and your business can only benefit. But there are some pretty important factors to consider when dealing with the wonderful world of online – the most crucial factor being you are not simply talking to your customers and potential customers who passively digest your messages. They are talking back. Reputations can be both made and destroyed online.

Crisis management

Also known as 'firefighting', the art of crisis management is one that many companies pay people millions of pounds to master, but few genuinely succeed. Crisis management involves turning a negative story or unfortunate event into a positive, or at least neutral, story or event.

What PR is not

We've talked a bit about what PR is, now a few words on what PR is not. Call it expectation management if you will, but it is important to be clear, at an early stage, on what you can expect to gain from PR, and what you cannot.

PR is not advertising

The crucial difference between PR and advertising is that PR focuses on getting brands and products into editorial space, which is a space that cannot be bought.

To put it very simply, PR is free coverage. Advertising is paid-for coverage. You pay your money, you are guaranteed a certain space in a magazine, newspaper or on TV on a certain date, and you are able to fully control what is printed or said in that space. With PR, you pay no money – and you have no control. You cannot guarantee where or even if your story will appear – and you cannot guarantee what the journalist will say about you.

The overwhelming advantage of PR over advertising is that everybody knows adverts are purchased. Therefore they are known to be vehicles of the brand or company that has purchased them, and consumers do not trust them. Editorial is known to be impartial – it has not been, and cannot be, purchased. Therefore consumers have far higher trust in editorial, and if an article says this brand or person is good, the public is more likely to believe it.

PR is not spam

At least, good PR is not spam. Direct mail and other mass-marketing methods are known as direct marketing and this is a different world to PR. Direct marketing can be a successful strategy and you may want to consider it as a part of your business strategy, but that is a subject for another book.

PR is not always easy or fair

However great your story, fantastic your photographs or dynamic your event, there is always a chance there will be a catastrophic event elsewhere in the region, country or even world that knocks your well-crafted, slaved-over pitch off the pages of a newspaper or magazine.

 example

The day Prince William and Kate Middleton announced their engagement, the chances of any other story getting on to the front pages of any newspaper, magazine or headlining any news bulletin in the UK were ruined. This was excellent news for David Cameron, the prime minister, who had earlier in the day removed an official photographer and film-maker from Downing Street's payroll. It was also good news for Take That star Howard Donald, who the same day was revealed to be the subject of a 'superinjunction' barring embarrassing allegations against him being reported. That day the superinjunction was lifted. But thanks to Wills and Kate, both Cameron and Donald would have been first in the queue to toast their happy news, as they had effectively escaped acres of unwanted negative coverage over their respective gaffes. It was not such good news for any brand or business who had a carefully put-together high-profile PR campaign set to launch on that day. The media was only interested in wall-to-wall Wills and Kate coverage, and many a good story will have been buried or never even seen the light of day thanks to them.

PR is an industry worth billions of pounds to the UK economy. The content so far does not do justice to this but it does provide you with the basic information you need to get started.

brilliant recap

- PR can be the difference between a well-run business that is struggling and a well-run business that is making a profit

- You do not need to pay a PR agency to build up a profile for you. You can do it yourself

- Editorial is more trusted than advertising, meaning it can make sense to concentrate efforts on getting editorial coverage rather than paying for an advert

- You cannot control what is written about you, when and how it is written. There are no guarantees with PR

CHAPTER 2

Where to start

The best PR is targeted and based on flawless planning. Teams sit down and work out the messages that they want to get out there in the public domain. For a supermarket like Asda, the message is value for money. For an airline such as Ryanair, the message is cheap and no-frills. For a department store like Harrods, the message is quality and exclusivity. People who shop in Harrods do not go there looking for affordable practical products. They go for aspirational products with a price tag to match, and they go for the kudos of having the means to be able to shop in the store.

It is preferable to use just one or two messages rather than a long list. Take Asda again – when you think Asda, you think value for money. Do you also think – quality products, great customer service, fantastic user-friendly shopping experience, home of the latest, most up-to-date products, organic, locally sourced, freshly produced, in association with celebrity chefs? Asda may well offer all of these things – I'm sure it does – but the messages from Asda always reflect its value for money. Just last summer, the company chose the first week of the Wimbledon tennis championship to highlight how Asda strawberries, which are from the same producer that is supplying strawberries to Wimbledon, are much cheaper than the ones on sale at the tournament.

Businesses with the best strategies pick one or two things that make them really stand out – their unique selling point or USP. This is not to say that a company that has chosen to make value for money its USP is automatically offering shoddy customer service and a poor quality experience – rather that consumers will quickly grow suspicious and switch off if a company claims to be the cheapest *and* the most reliable *and* have the best customer service *and* stock the most up-to-date products *and* so on.

It may be the product or service that your business offers, the nature of your client's business or the type of product you have to market, is its own USP. If you are selling or offering something that absolutely nobody else can offer, then your USP is already done and dusted. But very few businesses offer something that simply cannot be found elsewhere, and therefore they need a bit more thought to really stand out.

▶ brilliant example

Lucy Frankel, founder of Vegaware, which makes sustainable and recyclable packaging, on her USP:

'It really works in our favour being a green business, as environmental stories are very popular at the moment. It is a great help to be able to introduce yourself as working for "the UK's first and only compostable packaging company".'

For any journalist with a brief to write about an interesting or up-and-coming business, the words 'first and only' are crucial. The journalist knows they are writing about something that has not been done before, nor repeated since. A USP can be your 'news hook', providing substance, context and interest to your story and therefore increasing the chances of the media wanting to write about you, and the public wanting to read about you.

Identifying your USP

If you are a new business, you are something of a blank slate. You can use your business model, and the product or service you offer, to identify your USP. But often it is more fun – and a more successful strategy long term – to decide what you would like your USP to be, and build your communications strategy around it. Likewise, if you are launching a new product or representing a new business or client, you can begin from scratch and take the time to work out the best USP for your product or client.

First and foremost, you must commit to the USP. If you want price to be the USP, do your research first and make sure you offer a 'if you can find a better quote, we'll beat it' disclaimer to ensure you can guarantee you are always the cheapest.

When it comes to identifying, or deciding upon, the USP, think about what you want to be known for. All USPs have potential negatives as well as positives. It is vital you are aware of the downside to any USP you choose to portray, as once you begin dealing with the media and the public, you will have to be prepared to answer questions about it. How are you going to get around the potential negative issues?

If you are promoting a product or a client with an established business model and you have been unable to work with them from the beginning establishing the USP, then your job is to sit down and look at the marketing of that product or client to date, and pick out what you think is the USP. You should also be considering any negative side to the product or business, in the way described below.

brilliant tip

Imagine you are planning a USP for a food product or business. These could be:

1 Competitive pricing

2 Quality

3 Fast delivery

4 Delicious taste

5 Nutritious and healthy

But the flip sides of each of these could be:

1 Cheap and nasty

2 Too expensive

3 Slapdash

4 Unhealthy

5 Bland and boring

Ways to get around these flip sides:

1 Cheap and cheerful! No frills, no fuss, just the product at the best price.

2 Expensive, but you get what you pay for and you will impress other people by being able to afford this product.

3 We know you are hungry so our priority is getting our food on your table.

4 A little bit of what you fancy does you good.

5 This is a product that you can feel is doing you good.

Thinking about the potential negative connotations of the USP, and how to counteract that, is a useful first step to understanding more about PR. One of the great skills of PR is being able to find a positive slant to a negative story, or 'put on a positive spin', as it is more commonly known. Many PR professionals devote a good deal of their careers to developing this skill – with limited success.

Key messaging

Once you have decided upon the USP you may want to reflect more on the key messages you would like to get across. Key messages are an extension of a USP and help you tell people more about your business, product or client.

If the USP is price, the key messages may be 'you will not find a lower price' and 'no frills – just good honest service'. What we are aiming to do here is break down what the business, product or client can offer in short, snappy, simple soundbites. Think of any effective business and they will have key messages. To come back to Asda, who does not associate the supermarket with its infectious jingle and the patting of a back pocket filled with change? The message of value-for-money is intrinsic to all of Asda's marketing activity, and you can bet your boots this is one of the reasons for the supermarket giant's continued success.

Logo

The best logos really do speak for themselves. Think about Apple's logo or the iconic Nike 'swoosh'. You automatically associate certain characteristics with those logos. You know all about the product you are getting, simply by the small icon stamped upon it.

The best logos are also simple. You can say more about your brand or business with a very simple illustration or graphic than you can with a complicated, fussy design. It is worth taking time and investing in the design of your logo, as building up a brand identity from scratch is hard work, so changing the logo later on can set you back in terms of recognition and identity.

If you do not have strong feelings or ideas for a logo, it is also worth investing in a professional designer, or at least taking advice from someone with experience of designing logos. Brief them on what you want the logo to say about your business and any colour schemes or themes you want it to reflect. You may be surprised at other people's interpretation of what you are trying to achieve, and it can be an illuminating exercise to see what an outsider makes of your business proposition.

Colour is a powerful tool. Colours carry associations – red is bold, vibrant, fiery; blue is cool and clean; pink is feminine and delicate; and yellow is cheery and sunny. A black and white logo can work well, but coloured logos or using a colour theme can also be eye-catching and match the overall branding of a business.

 **example**

A classic use of colour is the Tiffany duck-egg blue. Anyone who has ever been the lucky recipient of one of their iconic boxes, tied with a white silk ribbon, will tell you the lasting impact that colour has had on them. It is associated with indulgence, pleasure, timeless beauty, precious gifts and expressions of love. Tiffany's website and marketing material all feature the distinctive blue heavily. That rich, inviting shade says everything about the brand.

Your brand

USP, key messages and logo all form part of your brand. I remember back in the 1980s when my mother, at the time a marketing manager, came back from a conference chatting about this new buzzword, 'brand'. Nowadays the term is ubiquitous.

Kellogg's, Coca-Cola, Nike, Apple, Microsoft and others are all as likely to be referred to as 'brands' as they are 'companies', 'firms' or 'businesses'. A brand is, in the most simplistic sense, the name of a company, product or service, but it is also the identity of that company, product or service. It is a combination of that company's logo or use of colour and design, the people within the company, the personalities, groups and organisations associated with that company, and the values the company stands for.

Nike is a brand, so is Adidas. Both produce sportswear. How do we differentiate the two? By their branding. The two have different identities, different logos, different messages, utilise different celebrities and personalities to act as the face (and feet) of the company, and endorse different sports, teams and individuals. All this activity forms the essence of the brand. A brand is nothing without consistent and creative activity behind it.

Think about a plain black vest. What does that vest mean to you? Nothing, it is simply a plain item of clothing. Now put a Nike logo on it and the vest becomes an entirely different proposition. It is quality sportswear. It is worn by the likes of Serena Williams and David Beckham. It means performance, stamina, speed, endurance, it wicks sweat, it keeps you cool in summer and warm in winter ... the associations go on. All those associations, just from a little tick. People attach values and attributes to a brand – a brand can be reliable, trustworthy, competitive, 'the best' – it is no wonder companies (or shall we just bite the bullet and call them 'brands') spend hundreds, thousands, even millions of pounds on developing their brands.

Building a brand takes time, and it takes consistent and well-thought out PR, often as part of a wider marketing and advertising campaign. Possibly the most successful brand in the world today is Apple. Put simply, Apple makes technology such as MP3 players, mobile phones, computers and laptops. Many rival technology companies also make all of these things. But Apple is different. It is time and again voted the coolest brand, the most innovative brand, the 'one to watch'. Design has long been a priority for the company, it makes products that are not only functional and practical but possibly more importantly, beautiful, tactile and stylish. The legendary white headphones supplied with the iPod, the glossy smoothness of the iPhone, the sleek lines of the MacBook, all give Apple products the 'wow' factor, turning them from everyday items into objects of desire and even cult status.

Apple did not invent the computer, the mobile phone or the MP3 player, but it did revolutionise all three products. A great deal of this is down to the company's ability to innovate and evolve, but its marketing also must take some credit for its current status as *the* brand of the moment. Its advertising has maximised on the brand values of the company and its products. The original iPod adverts were memorable and instantly cool, creating a genuine cult status for a product that was not in essence new. Its PR has managed to give the company an air of mystique, aloofness and general too-cool-for-school-ness. In the case of Apple, less is most definitely more. You will not see Apple spokesmen quoted in every newspaper and magazine around, but when CEO Steve Jobs talks, *everybody* listens.

Personalities

A company's CEO can be as much a part of the brand as the products or services that company produces. A good example is Michelle Mone, founder of the lingerie company Ultimo. Mone is an instantly recognisable figure, and stories about her company will more often than not focus on Mone herself as much as the latest product or innovation the company is promoting. Whether it is the unveiling of a new Ultimo girl or a stunning photoshoot, Mone's personality and vision is stamped all over Ultimo coverage. The result is that Ultimo enjoys a profile, status and cachet that other lingerie companies simply cannot compete with. It would be easy to argue that part of this success is down to the highly visual nature of lingerie and the fact that any product that appears draped over a Brazilian supermodel is going to gain column inches – but I wouldn't mind a small bet that more has been written about Ultimo in the last year than Gossard, for example. Mone is also active in the business and entrepreneur community, and her personal profile is as important as that of the company. She is her own USP and this is a very simple but highly effective PR strategy that has, in short, made her a fortune.

In an age where consumers demand visibility and accountability from the brands they purchase, having a noted, respected and known CEO is a huge advantage. When considering your overall branding, put yourself as head of your own business, or the boss of the business you are representing, in the mix too. What are your or their strengths? What do you or they bring to the business that nobody else could? Passion, dedication, drive and determination are essential in a business leader, but what else makes you or them unique?

And what about weaknesses, or qualities that others might consider weaknesses? Even these can be turned into a positive. Simon Cowell, Alan Sugar and Gordon Ramsay did not get to where they are today by being nice, empathetic and well-spoken.

 example

Think about the following well-known CEOs, from both the past and the present-day. What do you associate with each of them?

- Anita Roddick
- Michael O'Leary
- Tony Blair

All three are good examples of what can be achieved with a PR strategy that takes into account the personal qualities and characteristics of the person who is leading the business or organisation, as we shall see below. ▶

Anita Roddick was the original eco-queen. Without Roddick's strong beliefs and ethical stance the Body Shop would never have become such a successful and distinctive brand. The Body Shop was by no means the first company to produce beautiful-smelling cosmetics and products, but it was one of the first to tap into the desire of consumers to feel good and do good at the same time. Purchasing a Body Shop product in its heyday said something about you – it said you rejected overly commercial and glamorised products in favour of something that was right, fair and principled. Even when Roddick eventually sold her company to consumer giant L'Oréal, her reputation and image remained intact, all thanks to the power of her own personal brand.

Michael O'Leary, the legendary owner of Ryanair, is said by many to be a one-man PR disaster, thanks to his propensity for straight talking and his sometimes overly ruthless attitude to the competition and his own consumers. Ryanair as a brand has suffered its fair share of bad PR thanks to O'Leary's often controversial approach, yet the brand continues to flourish, and O'Leary's unapologetic stance makes him a consistent figurehead for his company.

Tony Blair – yes, that most controversial of characters still commands huge levels of public attention. The former PM was hailed as he entered Downing Street in 1997 and reviled when he left it 13 years later, but through good times and bad you could not dispute the power of his personality. To some a hero, to others a war criminal, Blair is a hugely charismatic and smart operator, and has redefined modern politics. The new politics is as much about personality and PR as it is policies and this is entirely down to Blair. He was the first PM to genuinely identify the power of PR and media relations, assisted by the original 'spin doctor' Peter Mandelson and Downing Street guard dog Alastair Campbell. Love him or hate him, you cannot ignore, or forget, Tony Blair. You only have to look at the three leaders of the major political parties to see the legacy he has left. They are all, as far as politicians can be, young, thrusting individuals with carefully managed personas.

The extraordinarily successful and high-profile individuals detailed above all demonstrate the power of personality and image, amplified by PR, in a modern world. We live in an age where consumers demand increasing transparency from their business, political and world leaders. The public wants to know what brands and companies are all about, and the people within those brands and companies are as integral as the products and services of the brand itself.

Your public persona

As the ambassador for your company, you must have 100 per cent belief in the product or service you are offering. As the ambassador for a product or client, you must have 100 per cent belief in that product or client – or at least be seen to have belief in it.

I once heard an illuminating story about a woman in her mid 20s who went for a job interview in the marketing department of a well-known alcoholic drinks company. She was a quiet, unassuming young woman who wanted to move into a more glamorous line of work, but came away realising the role was completely unsuitable for her, due to the company's insistence that she must 'live the brand'. She would have been expected to frequent bars, pubs and clubs, dress in a vibrant, trendy way, and order that particular brand of alcoholic drink whenever she was at a bar. In other words she was expected to, at all times, personify the brand – to be lively, trendy and intoxicating.

This is an extreme example, although the job of living a well-known alcohol brand would be very welcome to some. But the point I am making here is you must also 'live the brand'. If you do not show belief in what you are doing or representing, no one else will. If you make and sell bikes, cycle instead of walking or taking the train. If you are representing a fashion designer, wear their clothes. If you are launching a new food product, eat it. If you are an artist, draw beautiful things on your work notebook. Who is going to believe in a manufacturer who does not even use their own product or service? Similarly, you must also encompass the key messages of your brand. If you run or are representing a website detailing discount products and services, point out your bargain haircut, beauty treatment or outfit at every opportunity and do not turn up for an interview in Gucci unless it was purchased at 90 per cent off. All this sounds simple, but it is vital that you truly consider what 'living the brand' actually means. You are the best advocate possible for your business, and the public face of that business or your client or product, so do not let yourself down. It is surprisingly easy to do, as the following individuals prove.

David Cameron and the bicycle

David Cameron was a savvy PR operator when it came to the run-up to the elections. Which made it all the more surprising when the future PM, a vocal advocate of green issues, was caught cycling into work – followed by a ministerial car carrying his briefcase. His green agenda came under scrutiny following the revelation in 2006.

The ultimate PR gaffe – Gerald Ratner

It has been 20 years since jeweller Gerald Ratner committed possibly the ultimate PR own goal, but the incident serves as a stark reminder of the importance of demonstrating utter belief in your business, product or client.

In 1991, whilst addressing a conference of the Institute of Directors, Ratner made the frankly mind-boggling decision to call his own products 'crap'. He joked that his jewellery chain sold a sherry decanter that was 'crap' and added that 'a prawn sandwich' would last longer than a 99p pair of earrings on offer.

The upshot was Ratner's resignation and the company's value went down by £550 million, forcing stores to close. Ratner claimed he was being light-hearted and had no idea what contempt for his customers he was displaying through his comments.

At a conference at the Institute of Directors in 2005 Ratner admitted he still had not got over the incident.

Media training

It is standard for PR agencies to offer media training to the people they represent. This can range from training individuals, usually CEOs or similar, to act as spokespeople for their businesses and wider industry issues, to supervising an individual's entire public image and appearance.

Media training helps people prepare themselves for public scrutiny. PR professionals run through key messages with their clients, carry out practice interviews in anticipation of any questions a journalist might ask them, and generally advise on giving the right impression.

Watch or listen to interviews with politicians and notice how they remain resolutely on-message, sometimes in the face of intense questioning. Many avoid the difficult questions, simply parroting the same messages over and over again. This ability to dodge or not fully answer questions, developed through media training and a full understanding of which messages they want to get out, and which they do not, has given rise to the aggressive interviewing tactics of the likes of Jeremy Paxman and presenters on Radio 4's Today show, who attempt to fight fire with fire.

Media training is an investment which may well be out of your reach, but you can prepare yourself by considering the following points every time you are gearing up to talk to the media or the public:

- What is the key point that you want to get across?
- What overall impression do you want to create?
- What impression of yourself and what impression of your business are you aiming for?
- What questions might you be asked and how can you best handle them? Think back to when we were talking about USPs and turning negatives into positives. What positive messages can you put across? How can you respond to any negativity or criticism without sounding closed-off or defensive?
- Who are you talking to? Yes, a journalist, but who is that journalist representing? A local paper, a glossy magazine? Who reads or watches their product or programme, and how would you address them if they were standing in front of you right now?

Would *you* believe you? It is important to remain authentic. Whatever public persona you want to build – charismatic, likeable, authorative, inspirational, ambitious – you must be able to present yourself authentically. Play to your own strengths. There is enough room out there for business leaders fitting a range of profiles. As is so often the case with PR, one size does not fit all.

This may all sound very obvious, but your personal reputation may eventually be the most valuable commodity you possess. So it is worth taking the time to get it right. Even the best-advised people can slip up.

 example

Gordon Brown's 'bigotgate'

Arguably Gordon Brown was never going to emerge victorious from the 2010 General Election, but the final nail in his coffin was him branding voter Gillian Duffy a 'bigot' after failing to switch off his microphone. The lesson? Be careful what you say about the people that matter, no matter how insignificant your comment might seem at the time. We all get frustrated by clients, customers and the general public as a whole, but ultimately they can hold the key to your success (or failure).

There's a horrible saying 'Be nice to the people on the way up, because you never know when you might meet them again on the way down'. When representing a business or client, or your own business, everything counts.

 recap

- When planning a PR strategy have the USP, key messages and overall brand at the forefront of your mind
- A logo and use of colour can help to build a brand and say a lot about it with a simple illustration or design
- The CEO, founder or MD of a company are its public face and the best possible ambassador for it
- Live the brand and demonstrate belief in the products and services that you are offering or representing

CHAPTER 3

Understanding the media

About once a month, I get a call at the *PRWeek* features desk from an eager freelance journalist wanting to pitch a feature idea. 'How about a piece on what journalists *actually* want from PRs?' they ask. 'A guide for PRs on all the things they do wrong and all the ways they annoy journalists? What do you think?' What this little tale demonstrates is how crucial the relationship between PR professionals and journalists is – and how most journalists tend to feel PRs 'get it wrong'.

 **tip**

Media relations is arguably the single most important element to PR. You can have a brilliant, creative, well-thought out campaign with solid news hooks, celebrity endorsement, the works, but if you cannot persuade a journalist to run your story, then all your hard work will have been for nothing. Think back to the opening paragraph of this book – why are some companies consistently in the papers, whilst competitors with exactly the same product or service are not? Chances are, the oft-featured company will have a sound media relations strategy, and therefore when they phone a journalist with a story or idea the journalist will be more likely to pay attention.

In an age of constant, incessant communication, journalists are bombarded like never before with spam, nuisance phone calls and untargeted, unsolicited emails, tweets and messages. Separating the wheat from the chaff is a job most journalists simply do not have time for. As a result, many an email will simply be met with a click of the 'delete' button, and a follow-up phone call is most likely to never reach its intended target.

It is crucial, therefore, that you get your approach right. You need to give journalists exactly what they want at your first and subsequent points of contact. There are, sadly, no hard and fast rules – every journalist is different. But there are some well-established do's and don'ts that, whilst not guaranteed to get results every time, can certainly further your case considerably and help you stand out from all the noise.

The first step is understanding the different types of media and their specific interests.

Local press

Unless you are launching the next Apple, the *Daily Mail* is probably a too ambitious target to begin with. Instead, look at your weekly local newspaper. Studies consistently show that the public trusts local newspapers far more than any other type of media, and local newspapers have a dedicated readership. Getting a story into your local paper is the perfect way to begin generating local interest and signposting to the community that you are open for business.

 impact

Never underestimate how much loyalty, and respect, local newspapers command within the community. A local newspaper, far from being tomorrow's cat-litter lining or fish and chip wrapper, is a treasured resource for many, a source of constant information and entertainment. As a journalist working on a local newspaper I would receive constant calls about stories I had written, from people asking where this new shop was located or how they could go about taking advantage of an offer broadcast through a news piece. And here is a little secret – local newspapers are often pretty desperate for decent stories, especially smaller papers covering rural areas. Most local papers will have geographical 'beats' to cover and it can be hard work for a reporter digging out stories every week about a village with a population of 2,000. You can make the journalists' life a lot easier if you have a nice little story all ready for them.

Local newspapers are interested in stories about local people and issues affecting local people. They like human interest stories, court cases, inquests, accidents, successes, local activities and events, local organisations, history, celebrities and points of interest. If you can provide them with a story that features one or more of these, you are likely to succeed.

Regional press

Often beginning life as 'evening' papers, the regional press has suffered huge cutbacks and compression in recent years. I spent two years working at a regional newspaper which, when I started, published six editions each day from its head office and four satellite offices. By the time I left, it was down to just three editions a day and had closed two of its satellite offices. This compression has dramatically affected newsrooms. Once heavily staffed, many regional newspapers now operate on a skeleton of overworked, stressed staff constantly grappling to hit their many deadlines. Most regional newspapers now have websites that are updated constantly, further adding to the pressure on the reporting team. Photographers are another casualty of the reduction in staffing on regional newspapers.

Although sad for the industry, and for those working within regional press, this situation presents fantastic opportunities for PR-savvy business folk wanting to get coverage. Give an over-worked, stressed regional hack a decent story, together with suitable photographs, and you can pretty much guarantee that story will be on the website within the hour and in the following day's edition.

Regional papers are interested in everything local papers cover, but on a larger geographical scale. Given they cover a larger area, the story needs to be stronger to make it into a regional publication.

Commercial radio

Independent regional radio stations are increasingly few and far-between. Most radio stations are now owned by larger cor-porations, such as Global Radio, and a good deal of content is syndicated. This means that the late-night show you hear on your local station, is likely to be broadcast by many other local stations around the country. Syndication slowly but surely removes opportunities for local businesses – the opportunities that exist on commercial radio are really reserved for celebrities and pop stars. That said, most commercial radio stations will have their own, locally focused breakfast show and regular news bulletins, and these can be useful targets for promoting a busi-ness or product.

Commercial radio stations like brief news headlines, people phoning in to discuss issues and topics with the presenters, lighthearted banter and celebrity gossip.

BBC regional radio

The BBC really does have the monopoly on broadcast, and its regional radio is no exception. BBC radio tends to span a larger geographical area than the local press and this limits the opportunities for coverage. Very local stories are fairly rare unless they have a particularly strong news angle or are exceptionally quirky. Traditionally BBC radio has an older, higher-brow audience than commercial radio, making it a tougher target. The huge levels of trust commanded by the BBC however mean it is worth persisting.

The BBC has strong editorial values and a duty to provide licence fee payers with content that they are interested in and enjoy. BBC stations encourage listeners to phone in and interact with the presenters and cover issues that affect the region or the people living within it.

Talk radio

Talk radio does exactly what the name suggests. It is conversation and debate-based and focuses on a range of topics, from news events and happenings to irreverent and quirky items. Talk radio relies on interaction with listeners and features commentators and experts from the sectors which it is discussing. Although less popular than music-based radio, talk radio is an ideal target as it offers constant opportunities for people with strong views and interesting opinions. Some stations, such as TalkSport and LBC, focus on a particular area of interest or a region. Others are all-encompassing and will cover anything and everything as long as it is deemed to be of interest. Talk radio stations like expert commentary and people with strong opinions.

Regional TV

The news bulletins on regional TV programmes are always worth targeting, as TV remains one of the most influential mediums and certainly one of the most popular. But as with BBC radio, regional news programmes tend to steer clear from the kind of hyper-local stories that would easily fit into local press, and instead pick one or two key stories to look at in more depth. These stories increasingly tend to be event-based, such as a fire, car crash or crime in the area, or political. That said, there is always room for the quirky, 'rollerskating budgerigar' type stories, so bear regional TV in mind. Outlets are interested in national stories with a regional angle as well as stories that directly or exclusively affect the region.

National press

The Times, The Guardian, The Daily Mail, The Sun, The Sunday Times, The Observer and so on are all exceptionally desirable targets. That means that you, and the rest of the world, wish your business or client could be featured within them. Getting coverage in the nationals is possible, but it is a fine art, and not a task to be undertaken lightly.

brilliant tip

Expect to have to work extremely hard to get into the nationals, and brace yourself for the possibility that your phone calls and emails will be completely ignored. Most national newspaper journalists will not bother to take the time to say 'thanks but no thanks'. You need a thick skin to deal with the national press.

National TV and radio

As with national press, coverage on national TV and radio is possible, but exceptionally hard work, and you must be prepared for countless rejections, or simply to be ignored. If you are representing a small, local business, any coverage in national press, on national TV or national radio is an extremely unlikely, but not impossible, scenario. Try not to build your PR strategy around getting on to the nationals at first. Keep them as a desirable target, but until you are consistently scoring on a local and regional level, do not be disappointed if BBC Radio 2 does not leap at your pitch.

Consumer magazines

These are another super-desirable but extremely difficult target, although some consumer magazines are easier than others. Weeklies are an easier bet than monthlies, in particular women's monthlies, which are bombarded with PR activity from all angles. Coverage in a glossy women's magazine is pretty much the holy grail as whilst a national newspaper may take a critical approach, magazines are largely upbeat, positive publications and rarely say anything bad about any product or service they choose to feature. Readers are also hugely influenced by what they read in women's magazines, so if the beauty editor of *Vogue* says a product is good, women will rush out to buy it *en masse*.

Consumer magazines cover a myriad of sectors and interests, although the most-read tend to be quite generalistic in approach, such as women's magazines, foodie magazines and house and home style magazines.

Each publication will have its own areas of interest and there are no hard and fast rules for consumer magazines, so the best way to identify possible stories for them is to read at least three issues of the magazine you are targeting and be aware of what they cover and what they do not.

Trade press

As a consumer of everyday media, trade press may not really be on your agenda. Look deeper and you will find that for every profession, there is at least one trade magazine dedicated to producing news, features, comment and opinion about that profession. Case in point: *PRWeek* publisher Haymarket owns titles covering the wonderful worlds of windpower, printing and even caravanning.

Trade press tends to be respected within its sector, even if the wider public is largely oblivious. Trade press is always worth targeting, as in general it is far easier to get a piece in a trade magazine than many other forms of media, and the trade press does tend to command attention from those working within the sector it covers. Good trade press stories can be picked up elsewhere – stories that appear in *PRWeek* can get picked up by the national media from time to time.

Most, if not all of the above categories of media will have an online offering. Media websites range from constantly updated hubs of breaking news, views, comment, opinion and features, such as the websites of national newspapers, to basic sites which contain teaser copy from the media outlet in the hope that you will go out and buy the magazine itself. It is hard to give a detailed outline of the websites of media outlets, as they are constantly changing and being updated. To illustrate this point, at the time of writing, *The Times* had become the first national UK newspaper to put all its online content behind a paywall, swiftly followed by the *News of the World*. Whether or not this approach will work remains anyone's guess at the time of writing.

Blogs

There are more blogs out there in cyberspace than you, I and the entire population of London have had, or ever will have, hot dinners. The vast majority of blogs are entirely, utterly, fundamentally pointless for our purposes – they are simply websites housing the thoughts, views and rants of the blogger, and are often read by the blogger's mum and – that's about it. There are however a large number of significant, influential blogs, ranging from first-person accounts, such as the hugely successful Girl with a One-Track Mind blog from writer Zoe Margolis, to entire blog-driven news and lifestyle sites such as bitchbuzz.com. Blogs are as varied in tone, style, subject matter and content as is humanly possible, so decide which blogs to target, and make friends with those who write them.

Media relations

The rules of good media relations are relatively universal and apply to all outlets. You will need to tailor your approach to the individual outlet to which you are pitching, but first and foremost you must always remember some very simple do's and don'ts that every journalist you deal with will thank you for.

brilliant   dos and don'ts

✔ DO your homework. Read the newspaper or magazine, watch or listen to the programme you want to target, before approaching them. Ideally read or watch at least three separate editions. Find out when that outlet's deadlines are and avoid ringing when the journalists are likely to be up against it.

✘ DON'T pitch anything that will not fit into that media outlet's various sections or geographical beat. Find out what they cover and stick to that.

✔ DO pitch your story to the right person. If your story is about education, pitch it to the education reporter. If it is about health, the health reporter, and so on. If you would like to pitch a feature, take it to the features editor. And always ensure you have spelled their name correctly.

✘ DON'T phone up just to introduce yourself or 'have a chat'. Journalists are busy. It is not their job to find a story in piles of background waffle you have sent them under the guises of helping them 'get to know you'. Be targeted. Have a story, news hook or feature idea all ready for them – make their lives easier.

▶

✔ DO as you are asked. If the journalist wants a photograph or case study, do everything in your power to find one. If the journalist wants you to pitch the story by email, do it. If they prefer Twitter, send them a tweet.

✘ DON'T be a nuisance. Bombarding a journalist with phone calls and emails asking them if they need any more information or are they going to run your story is not 'being persistent', it is borderline stalking.

✔ DO accept that the journalist is in charge. It is your job to provide them with all the information they need to write their story. It is their job to actually write it and 'helpful' suggestions from you are not required.

✘ DON'T ever ask to see, or check, the story before it is printed or broadcast. No good journalist will ever offer copy approval unless you are an A-List movie star (which is why most interviews with A-Listers are so nauseatingly sycophantic). A journalist is a professional, writing stories is their job. They will check their facts as standard. The story will also go through an editing process, firstly by news or features editors, then sub-editors, then the overall editor. So even if you do get to 'check' a story, it still gets changed, altered and tweaked by at least three other people before it is published. Hence your 'changes' will be whipped straight out.

✔ DO manage your expectations. If you want gushing testimonies and a 100 per cent positive tone, buy an advert. Journalists are obliged to be fair, balanced and accurate in what they report. They are also not obliged to plug your business, print your web address and include your logo and corporate biography.

✘ DON'T try and be clever. Journalists do not have the time to jump through hoops for a story. They need information now so do not try and 'pique their interest' or any other teaser campaigns. Leave that to the PR professionals, who have limited success with these tactics.

✔ DO send journalists review samples and offer them access to your products or services without expecting anything in return. If they have the time and seem inclined, take them for lunch. Never expect any coverage as a result of this activity, but know that it will stand you in good stead and will pay off – next time the journalist wants a quote or has to write a review, they will think of you.

The above list is long, and only goes to show that the potential to 'get it wrong' is rife. If I had to break this list down to just one, crucial, vital point, it would be this: always be useful. Every time you pick up the phone or go to email a journalist stop and ask yourself: Am I being useful? Is my phone call or email going to make this journalist's life easier? If the answer is no, do not make that call or send that email.

The follow-up call

There is a practice rife among the PR industry that will never fail to provoke a long, vehement rant from any journalist – and every journalist, without exception, has been on the receiving end of this practice. It is known as 'the follow-up call' (although it is usually prefixed by a rather unflattering adjective by most journalists) and it goes something like this:

PR agency sends press release to journalist. Journalist does not respond within 12 hours. PR agency forces some unfortunate junior member of staff to make a follow-up call, which usually goes something like: 'Hello! How are you today? Isn't it a lovely day? I hope the weather holds out til the weekend! Anyway, I'm just calling to see if you got my press release. Was the story of interest to you at all? Do you have everything you need or would you like more information?'

The reason PR agencies force these poor unfortunate souls to make these maddening calls is because they reason that journalists are terribly busy people, and that they get hundreds, possibly thousands, of press releases every day. Therefore there is no harm in a quick call making sure their communication got through to the right person, and also in gently jogging the journalist into making a decision on whether or not they want to run the story.

The reason journalists will normally prefix a 'follow-up call' with some form of expletive is that the PR agency is entirely correct in assuming that the journalist receives hundreds or thousands of press releases every day. And for most of these press releases, the journalist also receives a follow-up call. That is a lot of bubbly young PR execs asking some stressed, overworked hack if they got 'my press release'. The non-specific nature of the call is one of its most maddening aspects and begs the blindingly obvious question 'Which of the one hundred press releases I received today are you referring to?' The journalist also reasons that if they had wanted further information they would have done something themselves, being as they are perfectly capable of clicking 'reply' or picking up a phone.

If you ask 100 journalists, it is my bet that 90 of them at least will say that follow-up calls are completely and totally unnecessary, and should be outlawed and punishable by death. So why do PR agencies keep making those calls? The answer is, much as I hate to admit it, once in a blue moon, the follow-up call actually works. Their press release did slip to the bottom of the pile, or had been forgotten, or enough attention not paid to it, and, as it turns out, there was a perfectly good story there which I may subsequently run. And without that phone call, it probably would not have happened.

Does this make the follow-up call worth it? I will not attempt to adjudicate. I will admit they occasionally work, but by and large they are a massive pain in the proverbial and I would happily never take another follow-up call ever again, even if it meant I occasionally missed a good story.

If you feel you want to make a follow-up call, then follow these golden rules. Say who you are and where you are calling from. Do not try and make irritating small talk unless you know the journalist personally. Say when you sent the release, what email address it came from and exactly what the story was about. Ask if there is any more information you can offer them. And then politely thank them for their time and put the phone down. If the journalist sounded like they wanted to throttle you, make a note not to make follow-up calls to that journalist again.

The best way to impress a journalist

Matt Cornish is the editor of a local newspaper and has worked for numerous daily and weekly publications. In his journey to the top of his profession, Matt has come across many a PR no-no, and here he shares his thoughts on the best way to get on his, and other editors', good side.

brilliant questions and answers

Why are relationships between journalists and PR professionals often so strained?

It may be a cliché, but journalists are very busy people. Often we're grumpy and unfriendly. This is because we're largely over-worked and understaffed. Our mood isn't helped by the dozens of calls and emails each day offering us stories which have no relevance to our publication.

How do you prefer to be approached?

Personally I prefer emails. But be warned, I receive 200 press releases a day, and I can filter the vast majority of irrelevant stuff very quickly. I delete most of them from the subject title alone. You ▶

get a sentence if the subject title hasn't put me off. Things that stop me deleting immediately are the name of my town, the word 'local' or something I can immediately recognise as being of interest such as the name of my local hospital, the mayor of my town or a local landmark.

Q What puts you off?

A Big name companies, car manufacturers, random non-local celebs in the title of the email. However, other publications may be interested in these and put off by my keywords, which is why you need to research first.

Q What can people do to get on your 'good side' and make you more likely to run a nice story or feature on them?

A Unless you have built up a relationship, don't pretend we're your best friend. We can see through overly chatty and friendly PRs trying to ingratiate themselves with us. We'll run a story if it's of interest to us and there are very few exceptions to this. Being efficient, helpful and relevant will get you a good reputation and are much more important traits than being friendly. That said, don't ever be rude as you'll get nothing.

Q How can people build up better relationships with you?

A Increasingly, I've been getting stories from Twitter and other social network sites. But it's not an exact science and relies a lot more on my vigilance rather than your efforts. I respond well to direct messages from people about breaking news, but from a firm I'd prefer emails. If you can build up a relationship with a journalist on a social network site, they'll be more willing to listen to you. Target journalists you may wish to pitch to in the future on social network sites rather than those you want to pitch to now. Talk normally and honestly about the issues they're talking about, even have debates with them (but keep it friendly). Only when they know who you are should you pitch anything to them.

Good media relations all comes back to preparation. You cannot research a media outlet enough – but you can certainly not research it enough. Obviously it's unrealistic to have a thorough grasp of every single newspaper, magazine, TV show and radio station out there, not to mention blogs and websites.

Instead, draw up a list of media outlets that are interesting to you and relevant to your business and have run stories about you. Subscribe to these publications and get to know them better. It is essential to include your local paper in there, as well as any regional newspapers and radio stations. Also include at least one national newspaper, to keep you up to date with the news agenda, and the trade and consumer magazines that are relevant.

If you can, and it is not overly distracting, have a local radio station or talk radio station on whilst you go about your day job. Or listen to radio whilst at the gym or working out. The more you listen and read, the more you will understand the targets you are trying to reach.

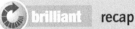 **recap**

- Media relations is arguably the most important aspect to PR and it is vital to get it right
- There are numerous different types of media outlets and each have their own agenda and areas of interest
- It is vital to thoroughly research the media outlet you are targeting before pitching to it
- Follow the golden rules, which have been put together in consultation with numerous journalists and really are universal
- Always be useful!

CHAPTER 4

Pitching

Also known as 'selling-in', pitching is the act of proposing an idea for a news story or feature to a journalist in the hope that they will run it in their publication or outlet. Pitching is a skill and, like any other skill, can be learned. But it is important to recognise that no matter how skilled your pitch, the chances of publication ultimately rest on the strength, or weakness, of your story. You can orchestrate the perfect pitch, but if your story has no legs, you will be banging your head against a brick wall.

What makes a good story or feature?

A good news story or feature needs a good, solid 'hook' – an angle that is topical and interesting enough to make people want to read beyond the headline. It is sad but true that the most popular news stories tend to involve a tragedy, a political blunder or a celebrity.

Assuming you are not lucky enough to have a celebrity to hand, and are fortunate enough not to have been involved in a tragedy or a political blunder, the following can also provide good hooks or angles:

- The wider news agenda – look for trends nationally that you can tap into or reproduce on a smaller scale, or offer comment upon as an expert.

- Local interest – particularly with local and regional media, having a local person or organisation involved in your story can be all that is required.

- The local/sector news agenda – issues affecting your particular area. Rural areas have different issues affecting them than urban ones, for example.

- Human interest – giving your story a human face, in the form of a spokesperson or case study.

- Events and activities – of particular interest to local and regional media as well as any specialist or trade media in your sector.

- Interesting quotes – a strong, assertive, bold quote can make a story. Do make sure you mean what you say though, and do not become a rent-a-quote (a person who will vociferously express their views on whichever subject the media outlet requires) as such individuals are rarely taken seriously.

- The quirky factor – an unusual or interesting event or happening, be it organic or manufactured in the form of a stunt.

- Imagery – a good photo can make a story, and strong imagery rarely needs more than the softest of news angles to make it into print.

- A good cause – if your business or story is supporting an organisation or charity.

- A rollerskating budgerigar – something so unique or offbeat you will not find it anywhere else.

The complete package

When you target your chosen journalist you will need to have the following prepared:

- A short summary of your story – one or two sentences maximum.
- A full press release with details of who to contact for more information.
- Photography and/or video content.

Summary

A short, snappy summary of your story is essential. This is what will pique the journalist's interest and make them want to read your full press release – conversely, this is what can turn the journalist completely off your story without bothering to read the full release. So it's important to get it right.

Abandon all jargon, fancy language and complex explanations. Break your story down to the absolute bare bones. What is this all about? Be harsh and tone down your ego where necessary. Remove all superfluous detail.

brilliant tip

If you are pitching a story about yourself or your business, try and remove your own ego from your description. Do you really need to describe yourself as 'Former City financier with an enviable client portfolio who wanted to take time out, spend more time with the family and pursue other interests and now specialises in bespoke aspirational catering, with Asian fusion a particular strength, for the discerning bride at affordable prices?' 'City boy/girl turned wedding caterer' will suffice.

The easiest way to master breaking a story down to a few basic facts is to read the newspapers, and pay particular attention to the introductory paragraph. The introduction is the summary – it provides the basic facts in the hope of encouraging the reader to read on.

Writing a press release

A press release explains the story, adds colour with quotes and comments and provides contact details for the journalist.

What you are aiming for is a concise account of the story, with quotes, over a maximum of two pages of A4. You can use the press release to anticipate any questions the journalist may have and answer them, but it is no reflection on your press-release writing ability if the journalist phones or emails with more questions. In fact unless the question relates to exactly when and where the story has taken place (fairly vital information), more questions from the journalist is a very good sign, as they clearly feel there is more to the story.

Begin with your introduction, which can be the same as your summary paragraph. Remember the journalist will want to know the five 'Ws – who, what, when, where and why? You can also add 'how' if you want, but stick to who, what, when, where and why and you will not go wrong.

Once you have summed up the five Ws, you can go into more detail, add colour and context. You should also include at least one quote, from a named spokesperson (yourself or the person about which the story relates). Once you have written your release conclude with 'Notes to editors' which as standard includes:

- a short summary of the company or organisation issuing the press release;
- full explanation of any figures, statistics or terminology contained within the press release;
- any FAQs you would like to include;
- full contact details including name, email address, telephone and mobile phone number of yourself as the person who can provide more information.

When writing your release good English is important, as is spelling, grammar and punctuation. Avoid Overly Capping Everything Up. I'm Not Sure Why People Do This. Perhaps They Think It Makes Them Sound More Important. It Does Not. ALSO DON'T BE TEMPTED TO WRITE ENTIRE SENTENCES IN CAPS TO GRAB ATTENTION AS THAT IS THE WRITTEN EQUIVALENT OF SHOUTING AT SOMEONE. Excessive punctuation! Should also! Be! Avoided!!!! All of these things make a press release harder, not easier, to read.

You do not have to write your press release as a news article, or in the style of the publication you are targeting. Your job is to provide the journalist with all the facts and information they need to write a story. Style, length and tone is down to them.

You can send a press release as an email or as a Word document, and here below is a relatively standard template you can use:

example

PRWeek features editor launches new book to help
small business owners manage their own PR

(Intro)

Cathy Bussey (WHO), London-based (WHERE) features editor of *PRWeek*, has today (WHEN) launched her first book (WHAT), a how-to guide for small businesses, those with a product or service to promote, or those new to the PR industry, to help them save money by learning to manage their own PR (WHY).

The book, published by Prentice Hall (HOW), aims to help small business owners maximise their knowledge of and passion for their business, and convert that into effective public relations leading to increased publicity for and interest in their businesses.

(Context)

The book covers an introduction to PR, where to start, media relations, pitching, effective PR campaigns and techniques, crisis management, online presence and how to choose a PR agency when the business is ready for more support.

The idea for the book came about after Bussey (see *Note 2*) began thinking about how basic PR skills are very simple and extremely effective, but not always widely known. Through the book she hopes to help demystify PR and show how business owners and those with a client or product to promote can, with a little help, achieve great results on little or no budget.

(Quotes)

'When people think of PR, they often think of sinister "spin doctors" and Max Clifford-esque figures, working behind the scenes to cover up the wrongdoings of politicians and celebrities,' Bussey says. 'In fact PR is an extremely effective business tool that can lead to greater awareness of a company, organisation, individual or issue. Good PR has the power to drive sales, raise a person's profile, even change the law.'

She continues: 'I hope this book will help people just setting out on their journey to realise that PR is not rocket science and that anyone can learn the basics. It is essential that small business owners know how to promote and represent their companies effectively and act as ambassadors for the brands they are building. It is also essential they do not waste precious start-up funds on expensive PR agencies when they are quite capable of managing their own PR. After all, who knows more about their businesses, than them?'

ENDS

Notes to editors

Cathy Bussey is a journalist with more than eight years' experience working on daily and weekly newspapers and magazines. She has been features editor of PR industry bible *PRWeek* for two years. She is represented by Isabel Atherton at Creative Authors literary agency. *Brilliant PR* is Bussey's first book.

Brilliant PR is part of the Brilliant series published by Pearson.

For more information contact Cathy Bussey: [email address and telephone]

For more information about Pearson contact [Pearson's marketing department contacts].

Note 1: It is up to you whether you want your story to be for immediate release or embargoed until a certain date. We will discuss strategic use of embargoes later on in this chapter, but unless there is a very good reason, for example, you are negotiating an exclusive or more in-depth coverage, embargoes are pointless and irritating – and sometimes broken, if the journalist feels there is no good reason for them.

Note 2: You will notice I have referred to myself here as 'Bussey' when quoting myself. This is thanks to years of working on business publications

▶

where the style is in the first instance to write out your first name and surname in full, and thereafter just use your surname. I could in this press release refer to myself as Cathy, Bussey or Mrs Bussey. Bear in mind most publications will have a house style and that will dictate whether you are referred to by first name, surname only or as Mr or Mrs surname.

All the above press release needs now is a colour photograph of myself and a colour shot of the cover of the book, and it is ready to go.

Imagery

Wherever possible, send an image with your press release. This could be a photograph of you, a photograph of your product or client or a photograph of somebody featured in your press release. Images are arguably more important than the press release itself – a good photo can make a story while a bad photo can break one.

It goes without saying that you need a digital image – the days of sending photos to be scanned in are well and truly over and really, who has the time?

You do not need to be a professional photographer to submit an image although newspapers and magazines do appreciate good quality photographs, so if you have the budget, paying a professional is a good option. If you do not have the cash, then make sure the basics are there. The photograph needs to be in focus and full colour, and needs to be an accurate representation of the subject. It also needs to be of a decent size, so aim for a file size of no less than 1MB.

Have a supply of 'stock' images that you can access quickly. This should include a headshot of yourself, a full or three-quarter length shot of yourself, and shots of your products and premises, if you have them.

brilliant   dos and don'ts

✔ DO ensure your photographs are clear, accurate and in focus.

✘ DON'T be tempted to be too arty, unless you are an artist or photographer looking to showcase your skills. Keep photographs simple and professional, especially photographs of yourself. No coquettish winking shots of yourself pouting at the camera, please!

✔ DO face the camera or stand at a very slight angle for head and body shots, and make sure you are in the centre of the frame.

✘ DON'T pose madly. A neutral expression or a smile is best. A good technique is to stand at a slight right angle to the camera, with your hands in front or behind you, and turn to face the photographer. This is a more flattering angle than facing the camera head-on.

✔ DO supply photographs in colour. Very few publications run black and white shots these days.

✘ DON'T send tiny photographs the size of a postage stamp. Publications need high-resolution, good quality images. Conversely though, do not send a gigantic file. One megabyte should be enough, any larger and you risk blocking the journalist's inbox.

✔ DO offer a selection of photographs, but send them one at a time to avoid clogging the journalist's inbox.

✔ DO touch up your photos if you have the equipment and remove red-eye. The art desk of the publication you are sending it to may also touch it up a little, mainly to improve the quality of the image when it appears in print. But do not ask, or expect, to be heavily airbrushed.

If a media outlet has the resources they may send a photographer to shoot you and your premises, products or anything else relevant to your story. Lots of people do not enjoy having their photograph taken and become embarrassed or awkward. Try to overcome any nerves or embarrassment. A good photographer should help to put you at ease, but do not be difficult or demand they shoot you in a certain angle or manner. They are the professionals.

Dress appropriately for your photographs and make sure you look smart and professional. You do not have to be suited and booted unless the photographer has specifically requested it, but ripped jeans and t-shirts with PORN STAR blazed across them are a no-no.

Video

Video is becoming extremely popular, not just on social networking sites like YouTube and Facebook, but also on the websites of national newspapers and magazines.

If your product, service or business lends itself to video, then you could have some short films shot that you can house on your own website as well as send to the media. Many media outlets shoot their own video or use specialist broadcast PR agencies. *PRWeek* shoots a weekly podcast, available to download on the prweek.com website, and this is done by an agency called markettiers4DC which provide studios, equipment and a presenter.

Video is an asset, but I would say at this point that it is not essential and is very much an add-on, unless your business is focused at the creative industries in which case you will be expected to showcase your talents. In general though, if your story is strong enough that the media outlet feels it is worth video footage, it should shoot that footage itself rather than expect you to provide it.

If you do want to pursue video, a hand-held Flip should do the trick nicely and many publications use them as a matter of course. A Flip will plug straight into your computer through the USB port and comes with built-in editing equipment.

 **definition**

'Going Viral'

The lure of video for many PR agencies, ad agencies and media outlets is its ability to 'go viral'. This refers to footage being passed from user to user either via sites like Facebook and YouTube or over email. If a video goes viral it has the potential to reach hundreds, thousands or even millions of people, for absolutely no cost whatsoever if it was shot at home on a Flip and put on to YouTube or Facebook. The paradox, for brands and creative agencies, is that what they would like to see go viral is branded content that encourages, promotes or in some way helps people purchase particular products and services. But the content most likely to go viral is videos of monkeys humping frogs, babies dancing to rap music, Hollywood actresses having sex or cats falling over. The challenge the advertising and PR world is grappling with is how to produce content with that instant 'share' factor (the monkey humping the frog) combined with the brand message.

Putting it all together

Once you have put together your press release, images and video if you are using it, it is time to pitch your story.

Whether this is your first pitch or your fiftieth, the rules remain the same:

- Find out who the relevant person to send your story to is.
- Ensure you have absolutely everything to hand before phoning or emailing your pitch in.

- Make sure photographs are of a decent size.
- Keep email size to a maximum of 1MB. Send photographs one by one if necessary.
- Include all contact details on your press release including email and mobile phone number.
- Keep your phone turned on and to hand to answer any immediate questions.
- Check that you are not pitching as the journalist is approaching a deadline.
- Be polite, professional and useful. If the journalist asks for something additional, do everything within your power to provide it immediately or as soon as humanly possible.
- Double check that you have spelled everything correctly, including the name of the journalist.
- Cross your fingers, take a deep breath, and pick up the phone or press 'send'.

More advanced media relations

There are a few techniques used in the media that you should be aware of. These are embargoes, exclusives, talking off the record and addressing the issue of 'misquoting'.

Embargoes

A press release sent under embargo means that it is not to be published or broadcast until the time and date specified.

Embargoes are very useful if you are holding an event or launching a product on a particular day or at a particular time and you want to notify the media and give them all the information they need beforehand, to enable them to run a timely story.

Journalists are obliged not to break embargoes. Some occasionally do if they feel a rival publication is in danger of 'scooping' them by reporting the event, launch or story first.

Only use an embargo if there is a genuine reason for it. Embargoes applied for the sake of it are extremely annoying.

Embargoes are not legally binding and you do not need to apply for one or follow any kind of formal process. Simply state very clearly that your story is embargoed until the relevant date or time. Make sure it is prominent, at the top of a press release in bold and repeated in the covering email.

Exclusives

All media outlets want stories and features that are exclusive to them and that no other media outlet has. This helps them attract and retain readers, by offering them content they can not get anywhere else. In a digital age when stories are broken on blogs and Twitter often way before they appear in print or in an online article, exclusives are becoming harder and harder to come by, and to keep.

If you offer a story exclusively, the chances of the media outlet in question covering it are automatically higher because they know none of their rivals will carry that story. Some publications, in particular high-end glossies or nationals, will insist upon an exclusive story or at least an exclusive angle as standard.

Conversely, some media outlets will immediately reject your story if they see they are simply on a long email list of contacts. For this reason it is always essential to email your pitch to journalists one at a time and personalise it with 'Dear X' and their correctly spelled name. If a journalist senses they are simply part of a mass mailout they will hit 'delete' immediately.

A wise tactic when pitching your story is to draw up a wish-list, starting with the publication or media outlet you would most like to get your story into and ending with the one that is least likely to be of benefit to you. Target the publications one at a time and offer the top-tier publication the story exclusively. If they come back and say no, you can take it to the next publication on your list, and so on.

If a media outlet agrees to run your story on an exclusive basis, honour that agreement and do not tout your story elsewhere until after it has appeared in the publication you have promised it to exclusively. If you do break an exclusive agreement, which is not legally binding unless you are receiving payment and sign a contract, you will be blacklisted by that publication or media outlet.

If you do receive payment and/or sign a contract then legally you are obliged to fulfil the terms of that contract. This is rare, as the only people who are paid for their stories tend to be celebrities and people who have had sex with celebrities, or people who have deliberately or inadvertently witnessed or been involved in an event of national or global importance.

Off the record

Talking to a journalist off the record means that nothing you tell them is for publication or broadcast, but for background information.

There are not that many circumstances in which you would need to talk to a journalist off the record. For a small business the only likely scenario would be if you are discussing information that is confidential to your business, to give the journalist the benefit of some inside knowledge and wider context.

It is down to you to state that you want to talk off the record. Anything said to a journalist is assumed to be for publication or broadcast unless explicitly stated otherwise. It is not the job of the journalist to ask 'Can I quote you?'

Therefore, if you are having a conversation with a journalist that you would like to remain confidential, state at the very beginning that you are talking off the record and nothing you say is for publication.

 **tip**

Anything you say to a journalist, no matter how informal the situation, is considered fair game for publication or broadcast unless you specifically state otherwise. By telling you that they are a journalist, the journalist has done their duty and does not need to ask for your permission to quote you. I am still amused, after eight years in the industry, how many people phone up outraged once a story has rung crying 'But I didn't know you were going to quote me!' I'm a journalist. That's my job.

Ethics do come into it however. If a person were to say something particularly inflammatory or stupid to me, perhaps unaware of how they sound as they are caught up in the heat of the moment, my own moral code would oblige me to ask 'Are you happy to be quoted?' That said, if what has been said is so juicy and scandalous that it will undoubtedly cause outcry, my moral code may be outweighed by my desire for a good story, and I may not speak up, leaving the poor hapless individual to realise afterwards what a mistake they have made. No one is perfect, after all. A journalist will sacrifice many things, ethics included, in pursuit of a really good story.

What about if you have talked to a journalist then realised afterwards that what you said sounds really quite bad? It is 50-50 I'm afraid. You can call the journalist and ask them not to use that quote and offer to provide an alternative, but they are not obliged to allow this and they may have already gone to press. It might be too late. The best tactic therefore is not to say anything that could be construed as wildly controversial in the first place, unless it is an explicit part of your PR strategy to appear outspoken or opinionated. And never forget that a journalist, no matter how positive a relationship you have with them, is first and foremost a journalist, and not a friend.

'I've been misquoted!'

We will discuss factual inaccuracies in the chapter on crisis management, but a note on the 'misquoted' phenomenon. People in general do not trust journalists, perhaps for the reasons I have touched upon above on ethics and a good story outweighing general human decency in some scenarios. But a journalist is obliged to be accountable and keep a record of his or her sources and conversations. Journalists take notes, either in longhand, shorthand, over emails or by using a Dictaphone. Therefore they should always be able to supply material that proves that what they have written is an accurate portrayal of a conversation.

True misquoting is in fact rare. A journalist is free to polish and tinker with quotes rather than reproduce them verbatim, in order to improve the readability or style of their copy. Therefore you will not see quotes with 'umms' and 'errs' in them, as these are removed for quality purposes. Quotes may be a shorter summary of a longer sentence or conversation. But a journalist is not permitted to attribute a quote to you that you have in fact not said, or alter the overall context of a quote.

A good journalist will never attribute something to you that is false, misleading or overly distorted or manipulated. If they have, you can ask for a correction or in extreme cases, threaten legal action. But in the vast majority of cases the journalist will be able to back up what they have written with notes or emails. For that reason it is wise to note down the general gist of any conversations you have had with a journalist and store any email exchanges you have had with them. Nine times out of ten, if you refer back to your notes you will realise you have not been misquoted, you just have not appeared in exactly the manner you wished. This is an inevitable consequence of media relations. You are not paying for your coverage so you cannot expect to control what is said.

 recap

- Have a news hook or angle and a summary, a press release, images and video if required all ready before you pitch

- Press releases should be in Word or in an email, not a PDF. Images need to be in jpg files and email size should be less than one megabyte. Send pictures one at a time if necessary

- Images need to be of good quality, full colour and high resolution

- Anything said to a journalist, unless specifically stated otherwise by you at the start of your conversation, is assumed to be for publication. It is down to you to say you want to talk off the record

- Exclusives can help you place your story as you are giving the media outlet something nobody else has

CHAPTER 5

Your online presence

t is absolutely essential for a business to be online. I cannot think of a single exception – whatever sector you occupy and product or service you provide or represent, there will be people out there looking online for that product or service in that sector. Not having a website removes any chance of those people finding you or the business you are representing. At the very least, the business, product or client must have some form of landing page where anyone doing a search can find out a little more about what the business, client or product does, and ways to contact you. If you are in the early days of running your own business and money is tight, it may be tempting to overlook the digital side of your business strategy, focusing instead on generating good word-of-mouth and hoping for referrals from satisfied customers. But even someone who has been given your name by a happy customer is immediately going to go online and Google you. A postcard in the local shop or an advert in the local paper will only get you so far. To succeed, you must be online.

There are entire books devoted to designing and building websites, and many extremely talented and creative web designers out there. Therefore this book will not attempt to usurp them and I strongly recommend that you consult a designer when putting together your site, unless of course you happen to be a website designer yourself. What we will consider is the content on your site or the website of the client or product you are representing, and how you can present it to the people searching for it.

 **tip**

When planning your site, think about websites you like and find easy to use, and those that you do not. Fancy graphics and videos look flashy, but often slow a website down and become irritating if you pack too many in. I am personally not a fan of the 'intro sequence' you sometimes find when visiting a company's website, when pictures and text gradually appear and disappear in sequence for thirty seconds or longer before you are given the option to 'enter the site'. Generally I find them tedious and time-wasting. That said, if you are a web designer or want to showcase your artistic merit, those seeking your services may be impressed. Think about what is appropriate for the service you are providing and if in doubt, go for user-friendliness over complex graphics and sequences.

What should be on a website?

Contact details

Utterly essential. If people can't contact you, they can't hire or buy from the business you are representing, and the phone book is as good as obsolete in this digital age. Postal address, telephone number and email address are a bare minimum, and if you or the client have a Facebook page or Twitter feed (which we will discuss in the next chapter) then you should also signpost these. Make contact details very easy to find. Put them either on the home page, or have a clear link to contact details from the homepage. People will quickly grow tired of clicking through link after link looking for a way to get hold of you. Someone once told me professional website designers have a 'three click' rule. If the customer can't find what they are looking for within three clicks of the mouse, they will not bother.

About the business/client/product

The main purpose of a website is to explain to people what the business or client offers, so they can make a better-informed decision about whether or not they would like to use the products or services on offer. Try and be clear, simple and succinct. Avoid jargon and over-professionalising descriptions. If you are representing a dog walking business, say so. Do not claim it to be a 'canine management solutions facilitator'.

If the business or client offers a range of products or services, you may want separate pages for each one, so you can describe in more detail what it is that they offer. Put a positive spin on products and services, but try and avoid over-exaggerated gushing. Stick to one or two well-placed adjectives wherever possible.

About the team

If the business has staff present them on the website to demonstrate the professional expertise they bring to the business. Keep biographies short and simple, and any photographs need to be appropriate for the role the person fulfils.

Clients, case studies and testimonies

Unless there are confidentiality issues, listing clients can be an effective way of proving the business is taken seriously by those who count within the sector. Examples of the work that has been carried out for clients, if the business is service-based, is helpful to showcase what it is capable of producing.

If a very high-profile client has said something nice about your business, or the client you are representing, do ask if you can put their comments on the website as a client testimony. Client testimonies can lend authenticity to an offering – if someone is prepared to put their name to an endorsement of a business or product, then others will feel more inclined to trust it to deliver on its promises. Clearly, everybody knows though that you are only going to put nice things that people have said on the website, as opposed to any constructive (or not-so-constructive) criticism.

News

A 'latest news' section on the website is a useful way of keeping consumers and other interested parties informed about what you or the client you are representing has been up to, as well as upcoming events and new launches. You can also use the latest news section to host press releases you have sent to the media.

If you are going to have a news section make sure you keep it updated regularly. Clicking on 'latest news' and finding a press release from 2004 does not give the impression of a forward-thinking, dynamic business. Ideally, update the latest news section at least once a month, even if it is just with a round-up of that month's activities.

A blog

Blogs can be a very useful way of sharing opinions and views, generating comments, input and opinions from the people you are trying to reach – your customers or the customers of your client – and building an online community. Blogs are generally less formal than press releases or news stories and allow you to express more of your personality. It is good practice to blog at least once or twice a week as a bare minimum. Ideally, aim for a blog a day. This will encourage people to keep coming back to the website to see what is new.

Photographs, imagery and design

The design of the website should reflect the brand and feature the logo and any colour schemes the business or client has decided to use. Photography of products and services should also be featured if the product or service is a visual one. If it is your own business you may also like to include a photograph of yourself, although this is not essential. Do pick a nice one! You can also use general imagery in the design of the site especially if you find imagery that you think says something about you or your business or client. A spa or beauty salon's website could feature imagery such as flowers, tranquil lakes and sun-kissed beaches, to signify beauty, well-being and indulgence. Take advice from a website designer when considering imagery to avoid making the site look cluttered.

Online sales

If you or the client you are working for are going to sell products online you need to make them easy to find and clearly signposted. Include a photograph of the product with a full description and price. You need to make it as easy as possible for customers to purchase them.

 impact

Selling online has the double advantage of being a great way to build up a database, as you can collect names, addresses and email addresses of customers. To encourage customers to return, a lot of stores set up personal accounts so that once the customer has entered their details once, they do not need to keep doing so every time they visit the site. Some more sophisticated sites retain credit or debit card details, under proper security, so that the returning customer need only click two or three times to go from start to finish. This makes it even easier for customers to buy.

Copywriting

Depending on how confident you are in your writing skills, and on how much time and budget you have you may either want to write the content for your or your client's website yourself, or pay a professional copywriter to do it. If you do opt to do it yourself, enlist a friend or colleague with excellent English and writing skills to proofread all of your material before publishing it online. A website littered with spelling and grammar errors will not impress anyone. In the case of a blog, you do not have to tirelessly proofread every entry but do make sure you have the basics right. It is off-putting wading through badly written and punctuated copy, no matter how compelling the content may be.

Your own blog

One of the great advantages of living in a digital age is that the ability to offer facts, opinions and comment is not limited to professional writers and journalists. Everyone can be a published writer now. Your blog can be attached to your main website or can be hosted on free software such as Blogger or WordPress.

You probably already read blogs yourself. There are so many out there, from the witticisms and observations of those close to political life to the rantings of those who feel disaffected by the media and the direction in which modern society is moving. There are few hard and fast rules of blogging, as a blog is very much a personal expression. But a blog linked and tailored to your business must follow certain criteria, as it is another part of your professional 'face'.

brilliant dos and don'ts

✔ DO keep it relevant. Anyone who has ever read, or written, a blog knows how incredibly tempting it is simply to spout off about whatever is bothering or exciting or irritating or inspiring them today. These kinds of blogs can be fantastically entertaining, but for business purposes arbitrary ranting is to be discouraged. If you are a person prone to strong opinions, keep them relevant to your business and the wider sector within which you operate.

✘ DON'T become overly emotional. Stay professional, even if you are really passionate about the topic in question.

✔ DO use your blog to discuss your business or work and issues relating to it. Share knowledge and advice as this will help you attract comments and interest from others within your sector. There is always a demand for balanced and insightful commentary on the issues you are facing which the wider sector might have to deal with.

✘ DON'T use your blog to discuss X Factor contestants and whether or not that celeb has had a boob job! You can do that on the *Daily Mail* website.

✔ DO remember your blog is a business tool and part of a business's public face.

✘ DON'T be selfish. If you are generating comments from people who want to discuss particular business-related issues, do so and do not ram your own business or clients down their throats.

✔ DO learn by reading as many blogs as you can.

There are also workshops for people to help them improve their blogging skills, such as the Oh My Blog workshop run by noted blogger Cate Sevilla, editor-in-chief of Bitchbuzz.com.

Driving traffic to your blog

Search engine optimisation

Search engine optimisation (SEO) refers to utilising key words and phrases that people are searching for online to drive traffic to your blog or website. Most blogging software offers you the opportunity to 'tag' keywords and by picking the right words, you will draw more traffic to your blog.

A post about being self-employed, for example, could include keywords such as self-employed, own business, small business and entrepreneur. That means that anyone searching for those words will eventually come to a link to your blog.

PR professionals spend a lot of time talking, and thinking, about SEO and how to draw the most traffic possible to blogs and articles that they are trying to promote. SEO is useful but as your blog is not your primary business, I would not spend too much time racking your brains over the finer points of it.

Links

On WordPress and Blogger, two very common hosting software, bloggers can link to other sites or blogs they like and recommend. If a fellow blogger has begun interacting with you on your blog, or complimented you on it, ask them to link to you. You can return the favour on your own blog, and this means traffic visiting their blog will see a link to you – and vice versa.

Occasionally the media will pick up on something interesting said or discussed in a blog, and online their story will often link to it. If there is a lively discussion going on around your blog, send a link to a journalist at your trade publication and invite them to have a look. Links also help boost your SEO.

Twitter and Facebook

Twitter and Facebook are both fantastic ways of drawing attention to your blog. Sharing a link on Twitter or Facebook (or both) means all your followers and fans will see it. We will talk more about about Twitter and Facebook in the next chapter on social networking.

Monetising your blog and being PR-ed to

Once you have a dedicated readership you may be offered the opportunity to monetise your blog, by allowing targeted adverts to appear on your site. PR professionals may also start to target you seeking coverage on your blog and offering you products and services to review.

Blogs can become helpful little earners on the side – figures of individuals who make money from blogging show the vast majority do so as part of a wider business or enterprise, not just from the blog itself.

There are bloggers and other individuals who feel passionately that brands and companies should not be able to advertise on or promote themselves to a blog. These people are in the minority though and most bloggers and readers of blogs recognise that everyone has to make a living. If you do choose to accept paid-for advertising ask that it is discreet. You may lose readers – and therefore the reason for the paid-for advertising in the first place – if you allow endless pop ups and flashing things to dominate your blog.

If you decide to accept products and services for review from PR professionals be transparent. Say that you have been sent this product and asked or paid to write about it. Readers appreciate honesty and do not like to feel they are being misled. Your readers are exceptionally valuable, they are customers and potential customers and the people with whom you want to interact. So look after them.

Online forums and networks

Online forums are hugely popular and house tight-knit communities that share and exchange huge amounts of knowledge and information. Perhaps the most high-profile online forum is Mumsnet, the hugely popular website for mums (and dads) which has welcomed the likes of David Cameron and Gordon Brown for live webchats. Such is Mumsnet's influence that the 'mummy blogger' audience – mothers of young children who are educated, have purchasing power and are active online – is often said to be the most valuable audience with which to raise awareness. Conversely, it is also one of the hardest audiences to reach with PR. The public, and mummy bloggers in particular, have become extraordinarily PR savvy in recent years. This is no doubt in part thanks to some truly shambolic PR efforts from individuals, such as hapless account executives who are forced to pretend to be part of the target audience in order to 'innocently' slip recommendations of products or services to their online pals. Online forums are probably more useful to you in a personal capacity than they are for PR purposes. If you can get a recommendation for your product or service in one of those forums, that is a great result, but it is hard to do and you will probably be seen through if you try to do it through trickery. All forums have rules that users have to follow. Stick to those rules and be honest, open and transparent about who you are and what your agenda is. Give as well as take – if you are asking people for help and advice with your life, business and issues, then do respond when they in turn ask for help and advice.

 **brilliant** recap

- Your business or client must have an online presence. In this digital age, it is simply bad business sense not to
- A website should reflect a brand and help people find out more about it, what it does, and how they can contact it
- Blogs and news feeds must be updated regularly to be of value
- Your own blog can be a useful business tool and even earn money in its own right

CHAPTER 6

Social networking

Social networking has revolutionised the way we communicate, consume media and interact with each other. It is not an exaggeration to say that, at the time of writing, the PR industry in the UK is justifiably completely obsessed with social media. The medium has the power to break news hours or even days ahead of any publication or broadcast outlet, influence the way people think, influence the way they shop and purchase, and can be used to call like-minded people to action in ways that are extremely efficient and also at times somewhat scary.

Social media also has one other, utterly compelling, advantage. It is completely free to use. Providing a person can access the internet, either through a computer or a smartphone or other device, they can use social media for no cost whatsoever. Were Twitter or Facebook to start charging users, the sites would be signing their own death certificates.

The main sites currently are Facebook, Twitter, MySpace, Foursquare and LinkedIn. I am going to talk more about Facebook and Twitter than the other sites, as it is my belief they are the most useful social networking sites currently operating for PR purposes.

Facebook

The 'biggie'. Facebook has, at the time of writing, some 500 million users worldwide. The site is growing and developing at a rapid rate and new features are being added all the time. There are groups, pages, events, applications, options for people to 'like' a status update, page, comment or product, targeted advertising and much, much more. As Facebook is constantly evolving it would almost be foolish to attempt to write a how-to guide to the social networking behemoth. Since I began writing this book Facebook has announced Facebook email and a new profile option for users. Suffice to say that Facebook's popularity does not look likely to wane any time soon. Therefore a Facebook page is a sensible PR option.

It is worth remembering that despite the apparent informality of Facebook, the site still represents your public 'face'. If you have your own Facebook page, you will already be aware that photographs you post can be shared among friends, and the wider public, if you have not adjusted your privacy settings. If you do use Facebook to connect with friends and post pictures of wild nights out, then do not use this account for work purposes. Set your privacy levels to the highest settings possible, and be careful what you choose to share. There is an entire Facebook group entitled 'Fired because of Facebook' and most people will have heard at least one horror story about a person being sacked from their job because of something they posted on Facebook – usually along the lines of 'I hate my boss, he/she is a bastard'. As your own boss, you are free to call yourself a bastard as much as you like, but a status update along the lines of 'Client X is driving me crazy' is not a wise move.

If you are new to Facebook, set up a personal account first and add a few friends and family, and take it from there. The best way to learn about Facebook is to use it, and by having a personal account with a few 'friends', you can experiment with the site and learn how it works.

As with planning a website, when considering a company Facebook page take inspiration from those you consider to work well, and avoid replicating the ones you do not find useful and engaging.

 **example**

Used correctly and in the right context, Facebook can achieve great things.

Wispa

Remember Wispa bars? Of course you do, because they are now back on the shelves of shops, thanks largely to an extremely successful PR campaign. Cadbury stopped making Wispa bars in 2003 due to declining sales. A Facebook group entitled 'Bring back Wispa' collected tens of thousands of fans and inspired many others, culminating in the company responding to the demand by relaunching the chocolate bar first as a limited-edition product, and finally as a permanent fixture.

The true picture is not as simple as this – there was a lot of clever marketing and PR behind the spiralling demand to see the chocolate bar back on the shelves. Rumours were leaked that Cadbury was set to bring back the chocolate bar, adding to the hype, and influential food bloggers were targeted to keep the momentum going. The campaign would also not have succeeded had it not tapped into two powerful emotions: nostalgia and the almost universal love of chocolate among the British public. A campaign to 'bring back X-brand Brussel sprouts' would arguably not have been so successful. That said, it was specifically Wispa that campaigners were clamouring to have back on the shelves, not another type of obsolete chocolate bar, such as Secret (remember Secret bars? Whatever happened to them ...). In this case, all the elements were there – there was an emotional connection to a product that was exploited and mobilised leading to a resurgence of sales in the Wispa bar, and a more protective feeling among the public about the bar – it had left them once and it must not be allowed to do so again. Facebook was not the exclusive conduit of this campaign, but its role was certainly front and centre.

▶

Rage Against the Machine for Christmas number 1

The coveted Christmas number 1 slot in the music chart has in recent years virtually been guaranteed to whoever wins X Factor, Simon Cowell's musical talent show that dominates TV, newspapers and the internet from late summer until December. That is, until 2009, when a couple from Essex started a Facebook campaign to prevent X Factor winner Joe McElderry topping the chart at Christmas with his debut single 'The Climb'. The couple, who appealed to those 'fed up of Simon Cowell's latest karaoke anthem' said they wanted to break the 'X Factor monotony', encouraging people instead to propel anarchic US rock band Rage Against the Machine's 'Killing in the Name' to the top slot instead. The track is best-known for repeating the line 'Fuck you I won't do what you told me'. Aptly, or ironically, depending on how you look at it, music fans did exactly as the campaign told them, and Rage Against the Machine did in fact top the charts at Christmas 2009, leaving McElderry's offering in second place. This campaign, driven almost exclusively by the Facebook group and amplified by newspapers, magazines, TV, radio and online communities picking up on the *zeitgeist*, again owes its success to an emotional message. The utter dominance of X Factor rankles those who object to reality stars, manufactured pop and Cowell's iron grasp on the pop music market, and it was those disgruntled many that made the campaign work. It is not thought that the US rockers were in any way involved in the decision to put themselves forward for Christmas number 1, although their popularity and profile certainly enjoyed a boost and they were the lucky recipients of the kind of PR money often cannot buy. They performed a free concert in the UK afterwards to thank fans for their support, and proceeds from the single were donated to charity, adding a 'feelgood' element to the whole saga and further emphasising the David vs Goliath, grassroots vs big business element of the campaign.

These two examples show just how powerful social networking through Facebook can be – it has the ability to mobilise huge numbers of people and unite them in a common cause, often at zero or little cost. Once a campaign has momentum behind it, the media will become aware of it, be interested in it and report on it, further fuelling interest in a happy spiral until a conclusion – usually satisfactory – is reached. But it is important to note that there are risks inherent in using social media – all social media, not just Facebook. The public is becoming very savvy to marketing and PR ploys, and unless a campaign appears genuinely authentic, rather than overtly driven by the company that will ultimately benefit, it will fail. This is true of all marketing and PR activity, but particularly online where the public can challenge, question and generally 'answer back'. For every Bring back Wispa or Rage Against the Machine for Number 1, there are numerous campaigns that have fallen at the first hurdle. You need only log on to an internet forum such as Mumsnet to realise that users will absolutely round upon any company that appears to be trying to use the community for its own gain. Every now and again a post by a hapless PR executive, along the lines of 'I've just discovered product X and it is absolutely brilliant, you should all try it' will be spotted and vigorously criticised.

What also made Bring back Wispa and the Rage Against the Machine campaigns so successful was their originality. There are now hundreds of 'bring back' groups on Facebook, including, amusingly, a group to bring back the website's own 'become a fan' button in place of the updated, but more controversial, 'like' option. It is hard to see all of the products and services 'fans' are clamouring for on Facebook making a triumphant, Wispa-esque return. Or will 2011 see a Christmas number 1 along the lines of 'Killing in the Name'? At the time of writing, who knows – but it is unlikely that anyone will repeat the success of the Rage Against the Machine effort. Rather, a new and innovative campaign will emerge in its place.

Twitter

The 'newbie', Twitter has at the time of writing in excess of 75 million users, making it a baby in comparison to Facebook, but nonetheless a force to be reckoned with. Twitter allows users to post short updates – 140 characters or less – as regularly as they want. Users 'follow' other users, which means they choose to receive updates from these users in their news feed. Users can also search for individuals, companies and brands and view their updates (Tweets), unless that user has chosen to protect their Tweets. Although many do protect their updates, it is largely considered good practice if you want to build up a decent following to make them available to all. Users can communicate with each other and respond to Tweets publicly, using an '@' reply, or via a direct message, again in 140 characters or less.

As with Facebook, when using Twitter remember anything you post is pretty much fair game. Even if you protect your Tweets, which is not a recommended strategy when using Twitter to promote yourself, your business or your client, there is nothing to stop one of your followers repeating – or retweeting, as it is known – your updates. Therefore as with Facebook, avoid the 'Client X is a bastard' updates, for obvious reasons.

Twitter differs from Facebook considerably, as users are generally limited to posting 140-character updates, although these can include links to websites, articles or blogs via short links. Services such as bit.ly, for example, have evolved to shorten web addresses, so the user does not need to waste all 140 characters on a long and involved URL. Through services like Twitpic users can also post pictures, and Twitter updates can be linked to Facebook status updates and Foursquare.

Twitter and news outlets

More and more people are getting their news from Twitter. The site has so many users in so many privileged positions that it is now almost *de facto* for a journalist from a national newspaper to tweet a story ahead of breaking it online or in the publication. Rumours that begin on Twitter very often turn out to be true. A case in point: a few weeks ago I noticed somebody tweeting that Chris Hughton, at the time the manager of Newcastle United, was to be sacked. Within two hours the rumour, which came seemingly from nowhere, was confirmed to be true and a statement was put up on the club's website. In pre-Twitter days, the first any Newcastle United fans would have heard about it would be a story online, on TV or on the radio. But by the time the Hughton story made it online or on to TV or radio, many people already knew all about it.

There are always exceptions – spoof stories such as the Jeff Goldblum is dead rumour that persisted on the site for months and months. There's also a lot of unfounded speculation on Twitter, mainly about Premiership footballers, superinjunctions and pregnant teenagers. The more you use the site the more you learn to separate the wheat from the chaff.

Using Twitter

The site is exceptionally useful for connecting with large numbers of people in a succinct and comprehensive manner. There is something of an art to Tweeting and it takes time to get used to saying everything you want to say in 140 characters. The best Twitter accounts are those that people enjoy interacting with.

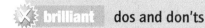

brilliant   dos and don'ts

✔ DO post frequently. If you only go on Twitter once a month you will not generate any interest. You need to be posting daily at least.

✘ DON'T post what you had for lunch. This is a cliché, but your posts need to be interesting and relevant if you want people to follow you.

✔ DO learn from your posts. If an observation leads to several people replying to you, retweeting and generating you new followers, then consider it successful. Shortening links through sites like bit.ly also allows you to see how many people have clicked on those links. If a lot of people clicked on your link, then that was a useful exercise.

✘ DON'T be afraid to use humour. Your goal is to raise awareness of yourself and your business, but the average Twitter user will respond well to being entertained.

✔ DO learn from other people using Twitter, particularly those who have lots of followers. What are they doing and how can you emulate them?

✘ DON'T be too self-promoting. No one will criticise or condemn you for talking about what you are up to, your business and your new products and services. But try and keep a balance and do not just post a stream of links to your blog and website.

✔ DO make observations, such as links to newspaper articles with topical or relevant information, and other blogs you find interesting.

✘ DON'T be too businesslike. Try and remain friendly and approachable wherever possible. Asking questions, encouraging responses and interacting with others will all help you present yourself as an approachable human being, not a faceless executive.

✔ DO thank anyone who compliments you or your products and services on Twitter.

✘ DON'T attention-seek. Think about the girl on Facebook who regularly posts 'Oh, I'm so fat and awful' so her 'friends' will immediately rush to clamour 'No, you're not, you're gorgeous!'. People will quickly grow tired of this kind of fishing for attention and compliments.

✔ DO retweet other people if you have found their comments and links interesting or useful.

✘ DON'T titillate unless you are working in the sex industry. If you are lucky enough to work as a model and want to use Twitter and Facebook to raise your personal profile it is fine to post portfolio pictures of yourself, but unless you are an underwear model 'arty' black and white shots of you pouting in your knickers will probably not generate the response you are after!

Followers and following

If you find a person, regardless of status and celebrity, interesting then follow them. Do not expect this to lead to a personal relationship – you can '@' Stephen Fry all you like but he is very unlikely to invite you round for dinner. I have noticed an increasing trend for people to ask celebrities and people with large followings to retweet their appeals for fundraising donations and other charitable causes, which is fine and many do oblige, but again, do not assume this means you are now bosom buddies.

You can search Twitter and find people who are posting about things you are interested in. For example, if you are interested in cycling, a Twitter search for 'cycling' will bring up tweets mentioning cycling, and you can take a look at that person's profile page and decide if you want to follow them.

Media sources, journalists and writers are always worth following as they will usually tweet news before it breaks, quickly followed by a link to a news story. As we have discussed, 'breaking' news is usually old news on Twitter by the time it appears anywhere else. Beware rumours though, and spoofs – Jeff Goldblum is not, repeat NOT dead. At least, not at the time of writing.

Journalists often tweet when they are looking for help with an article or case studies, as do PR professionals.

Many celebrities, brands and businesses have Twitter accounts, and you can follow these to keep up to date with their news and views. Again, beware the spoofs – there are hundreds of thousands of spoof Twitter accounts out there, some of which are very funny and worth following just for a giggle, but a genuine Twitter account will often be 'verified' by Twitter, so you know you are following the actual Lady Gaga, not a prankster.

You do not have to follow everyone who follows you. Only follow people you find actually interesting, useful or entertaining.

In terms of followers, clearly the more the merrier. The best way to generate followers is to update your Twitter feed frequently, with interesting and entertaining tweets, and interact with other users, replying to their updates where appropriate. The more you use Twitter, the more people will become aware of you.

Hashtags

Twitter can sometimes seem like a children's playground, with everybody all shouting at the same time. Hashtags exist to help people find tweets about a particular topic. So for example, if you are watching X Factor and want to discuss it with other people on Twitter, you can add the hashtag #xfactor to the end of your tweets. Anyone searching for the X Factor hashtag will then find your tweet, along with all the other tweets about the programme that have used the hashtag.

Every Friday Twitter users recommend people to follow to their network of followers, using the hashtag #followfriday or #ff. This is a nice tradition and one which you should use, as by recommending interesting people to follow, you are providing a service to your own followers. It is also good manners for those who receive a recommendation from you, to recommend you back – although this does not always happen.

Some people use hashtags comically, so they may tweet something like 'I have a headache #dranktoomuchlastnight'. You will see people doing this quite a lot on Twitter and it is less for search value and more for comedy value.

 example

Many businesses using Twitter offer their products or services to, for example, the first five people who retweet them. This is hugely effective in engaging with your followers and making them feel it is worth following you and also in raising wider awareness of who you are and what you do.

LinkedIn

Networking site LinkedIn has around 80 million registered users. It allows users to build up their own networks and join groups of like-minded people for discussion. LinkedIn tends to be used by professionals, for professional purposes, as opposed to Twitter and Facebook which are used probably more for entertainment than they are for professional purposes. This limits LinkedIn's reach but also means you are talking to people who are less likely to be Lol-ing and flirting and more likely to be genuinely interested in your business.

The site lets people put together their own networks, search and apply for jobs, find out more about a particular company or business, and find business opportunities. Users can also post questions for the community to answer, and recommend products and services. Like Facebook, LinkedIn is evolving all the time and the best way to get to know it is to use it. It is my personal view that the site is more useful for business and professional development, than for purely PR purposes.

Foursquare

Foursquare allows users to share their locations. Users 'check in' at certain locations, using GPS on smartphones, and can then access tips, information and advice others have left about that location. So somebody checking in at a museum, for example, may see other users have recommended particular exhibits to visit or ways to beat the queues, or warned that the escalators are out of service. Users can make 'friends' with other users on Foursquare, so can then 'shout out' to see if any of their friends are nearby. Foursquare can also be linked to other social networks, like Facebook and Twitter, so individuals can see where their friends are.

If an individual visits a certain location often enough they become 'mayor' of that location. This in itself does not carry any benefits but some brands use this as a promotional activity. For example, coffee shops may offer their 'mayors' some free products. This encourages repeat custom, and shows that the brand or business rewards loyalty.

Location and mobility

I mentioned at the beginning of this chapter that social media has the power to mobilise large numbers of people. This began with mobile phone technology, viral email and social networks with the 'flash mobs' that became popular for a while, where large amounts of people would go to a certain place at a certain time and perform a certain activity, such as dance to music on their iPods.

PR companies have attempted to reproduce this mobility, by organising their own flash mobs, but the general consensus is that the brand or business gets lost within the story. One famous PR stunt involved a large amount of girls dressed up as Beyoncé performing a dance to her single 'Single ladies in Piccadilly Circus'. Everybody who saw or read about that stunt will remember the dancing girls but who remembers that the brand involved was Trident chewing gum?

Some of the best examples of social media mobilising large numbers of people have nothing to do with planned or organised PR at all. Think about the violent student protests at the end of 2010, when students used every means available to them, including Twitter, Foursquare and live Google maps, to act as a united group against a rise in tuition fees. No PR company could tap into organisation and motivation on this scale, for a simple brand.

However the PR profession remains excited about location-based technology. It is thought that in the next year or two applications like Foursquare and Facebook Places will come into their own. Users will become more comfortable about sharing their location and information, if they feel they are going to receive something useful in return. That could be products or services, an experience or information. The PR industry is increasingly gearing up to service a generation characterised by indecisiveness and impatience. Mobile phones and social networking have made long-term plans unnecessary and obsolete. Instead, the thinking goes, people, especially younger consumers, are looking to be instantly entertained and gratified and if they are not, they will use the technology at their disposal to move elsewhere and onto the next thing.

A note on internet speak

Lol! Rofl! PMSL! I can haz? Confused – you should be. The internet is full of abbreviations, quirks, acronyms, emoticons and online speak. By and large, as a business professional, you do not want to be ROFLing too often ☺. It is worth becoming *au fait* with the more common abbreviations, and you can occasionally throw a Lol into the mix should you so desire, but a Twitter feed or blog full of gibberish, smiley faces and numbers instead of letters will smack of teenage girl, not successful business owner. Lol!

 **recap**

- Social networking is a powerful tool that can have massive impact and is free to use
- Twitter, Facebook, LinkedIn and Foursquare are as much extensions of your public face as any other promotional activity
- Social media involves give and take – you cannot talk exclusively about yourself and your business and expect to get results
- Avoid internet speak

CHAPTER 7

Creating a campaign

B roadly speaking, a campaign is a series of marketing and publicity-related activities that link together to meet specific objectives.

Campaigns can be based upon PR alone, and many are, or can incorporate other marketing disciplines such as advertising and direct marketing. Campaigns incorporating more than one marketing discipline are usually referred to as 'integrated campaigns'.

 **example**

The following examples are campaigns nobody could forget or ignore.

Hello Boys

Who can forget the iconic Wonderbra campaign, in which Eva Herzigova literally stopped traffic with her ample and well-supported assets.

The Hello Boys campaign combined advertising and clever PR. The strategically placed billboards and posters that formed the main element of the campaign were complemented by a PR strategy including reports of transfixed drivers screeching to a halt to gaze in awe at Herzigova's chest. The campaign worked because it was obviously sexy and fun, but did not alienate women, as it allowed them to believe they too could possess this power over men and transform their cleavages into pneumatic, Herzigova-esque traffic-stoppers. The campaign generated buzz across all sections of

▶

the media and Wonderbra became a lifestyle choice more than a simple piece of underwear.

Since 'Hello Boys' many other brands and organisations – including, terrifyingly, the Conservative Party – have tried to recreate Hello Boys, but the original will always remain the best. Hello Boys was a one-off, so the challenge for brands is to think of something equally creative – but new.

Comparethemeerkat.com

When car insurance comparison site Comparethemarket.com launched its latest campaign, including advertising and PR, even it may not have foreseen the success it has enjoyed. The concept was simple and silly – a Russian meerkat creates a series of TV and radio advertisements complaining that traffic intended for Comparethemarket.com is ending up at his site, comparethemeerkat.com. The campaign was supported with an actual site that compared meerkats, and has spiralled to the point where Aleksandr Orlov, the meerkat in question, has his own autobiography riding high in the UK book charts. The fictional character has also been interviewed by legitimate media outlets.

The success of Comparethemeerkat can be put down to great creative advertising and PR. The idea is brilliant – funny, irreverent and endlessly British. Giving the meerkat a Russian accent is also a stroke of genius and adds to the general silliness of the campaign. In fact the creation of Aleksandr Orlov, along with his website, book, Twitter account, Facebook page and goodness knows what else, may have entirely eclipsed the site he is meant to promote – but it is unlikely that Comparethemarket.com will mind.

The iconic campaign has sparked offerings from rival comparison sites like Go Compare and Moneysupermarket.com and perhaps tellingly both have chosen a rather silly campaign with a leading character with a foreign accent. Imitation is the sincerest form of flattery, and Comparethemarket. com will be laughing all the way to the bank thanks to Aleksandr.

Why run one?

The examples above detail some truly brilliant campaigns that have, simply put, transformed the fortunes of a brand. Before Hello Boys, Wonderbra was virtually unknown, and before Comparethemeerkat, Comparethemarket.com was just another price comparison website. These campaigns did not simply help sell a product or service, they helped propel the brands into the spotlight and have established them a genuine heritage. Wonderbra now has an eternal cachet that other push-up bras, no matter how effective, will struggle to match. Likewise, despite rivals adopting comical foreign-accented characters to front their campaigns, the success of Comparethemarket.com's campaign has propelled it streets ahead in terms of image and reputation.

A great campaign can make a brand. As we will discuss, you do not necessarily need a vast budget, or even any budget at all, to run an effective campaign which, if not quite on the scale of Hello Boys, can certainly give you a real boost.

If your PR experience to date has been limited to pulling together a story, phoning the relevant journalist and seeing or hearing the fruits of your efforts, then you are on the right track. This hit-by-hit approach is clearly working for you, and you should feel justifiably proud.

But as with any aspect of business, if you want to grow and improve your business, you must grow and improve your skills, and this includes growing and improving your PR. And if you are working for a client or promoting a product, running a PR campaign is an essential part of your job. A properly thought-out and executed PR campaign can not only boost your or your client's public profile, but also have a positive impact on referrals, inquiries and crucially, sales.

Planning a campaign

When beginning to plan your campaign start at the end. What do you want to achieve? Perhaps you are looking to:

- boost your public profile;
- raise awareness of your business or client;
- associate your business or client with a particular cause or organisation (for example, a charity);
- drive traffic to your or your client's website;
- increase your or your client's presence across social media;
- increase inquiries;
- drive sales.

 **tip**

Whatever objectives you set for yourself, they are what you will ultimately be measuring your success against. Think carefully and be realistic. Unless you are planning on bringing in a professional PR agency and allowing them free rein with a not-inconsiderable budget, a target of coverage in all the nationals and increasing sales by 200 per cent is probably a stretch too far at this stage.

It helps to be as specific as possible with objectives. There may be an aspect of your business or client's business you want to promote and generate interest in, such as a new product. Or you may want to establish yourself or your client as an industry spokesperson by targeting trade press. Or draw attention to your blog or increase your number of followers on Twitter.

Target audience

Think about who you want to reach with your campaign. Do you want to raise awareness among a particular audience, such as mums with young children or commuters? If you have a target audience in mind, you must tailor your activity to appeal to the kind of media these people are more likely to consume. Young, fashion-conscious women might not read the *Financial Times*, but you will probably get their attention if you manage to get a piece in *Cosmopolitan*.

Many PR professionals put together media lists at the start of their campaigns, outlining which outlets they would like to get their story into – and which they are likely to be able to get their story into.

You may find it helpful to draw up a media list for your target audience, including newspapers and magazines, TV and radio, blogs and websites. This will help you focus your pitching. Make sure you are familiar with all the media outlets you are hoping to target – the usual rules apply, do your homework, read or watch the product, and find out who is the right person to pitch to.

Budget

How much are you or your client prepared to spend on the campaign?

Think about your own time – how much of your time are you willing to or being asked to put into the project? Will you look for a freelancer or assistant to help you out and if so, how much are you willing to pay them?

Think also about the financial impact if it is your own business. Promotions such as vouchers, discounts and money-off initiatives can be effective at getting people through the door, but decide how much you are prepared to discount and stick to that figure.

The wider news agenda

One of the most obvious, and the most effective, ways to generate maximum publicity is to tie your campaign into the wider news agenda. This is simply an extension of identifying a news hook for an individual story.

 **tip**

The economic climate, as gloomy as it is, could be an ideal hook if you want your campaign to promote the fact that your business offers value for money. Tailoring events, stunts and activity to the wider theme of saving your consumers money could prove an effective strategy. A series of vouchers, special offers and other promotional activity might find a willing audience if tied in with a 'beat the recession, beat the cuts' style message, and if you persuade the cash-strapped consumer that you are on their side.

Awareness days, weeks and even months provide a great opportunity for you to hang your coat-tails on to a national campaign. The media will already be tuned in to that particular cause or subject matter, so it should be easier to work your way in. Many charities run awareness events for their particular cause and activity supporting this can help you with your own PR too.

Awareness days and weeks have a far wider reach than charity. Ever heard of National Bike Week? Or National Chip Week? If you are a representing a cycling company or a fish and chip shop, it simply makes sense to capitalise on these awareness weeks by planning activities such as open days, discounts, special offers, in-store events and other promotional activity.

The flip side is that there is an awareness day or week for just about anything these days, and the media is a little saturated with them. Many of the more obscure ones (Orangutan Awareness Week) slip by with little or no attention paid to them. So choose your cause carefully. Think about the audience you are trying to reach, and choose a week or event that will resonate with them. Going back to our fashion-conscious women target, you could run special events around Fashion Week, as the spotlight turns firmly on home-grown talent. This means the media will be much more inclined to write about up-and-coming fashion brands, and that fashion-conscious individuals will be eagerly scanning newspapers and magazines for fresh ideas and thinking.

Activity

Press releases and news stories

A series of press releases does not a campaign make. However, you will want to let the media know about the activity you are planning so a series of press releases launching the campaign, explaining each event or activity in depth, and then rounding up the campaign should be put together, along with photographs where possible.

If your campaign is attached to a particular cause or theme – for example, it ties in with a charity initiative or a news-related theme such as the recession – consider if you could use case studies or spokespeople. Giving a story a human face makes it so much easier to place.

Stunts

Stunts are usually expensive, and therefore out of the budget range of most businesses. Stunts also run the risk of becoming the story, at the expense of the brand or business itself. However technology and social media has made it easier for businesses to carry out low-budget stunts.

 **example**

On 14 October 2010 Greater Manchester Police tweeted every single call the force received over a 24-hour period. The idea was to showcase the varied nature of modern policing, ahead of anticipated brutal public sector funding cuts. The three feeds used by the police force peaked at 17,000 followers and the stunt generated a huge amount of online and offline coverage. Twitter is free to use, so the coverage was achieved with zero budget other than staff time.

Events

Never underestimate the power of events. They are a way to get people through your or your client's door, network and meet current and future clients, as well as make valuable links with other businesses in your area or sector.

The point of your event is to showcase yourself and your business or client, but you want participants to be engaged in some way rather than simply milling around.

If you are going to hold an event, do it properly. Publicise it, plug it and work hard to make it the best it can possibly be. People remember enjoyable events – and they do not forget bad ones either.

Whether you are holding an open day, a workshop, a brainstorming session or a fundraiser, greet everybody with a smile, hand out business cards galore, speak to as many people as possible and remember to take the time to enjoy the whole thing. Send press releases to relevant media at least a week in advance of your event, to help them plan. After the event, send a follow-up release to everyone you invited, detailing how many people attended, what went on and provide photographs. Photographs of children getting involved in fun events will always go down well, but make sure you have permission first from the parents to photograph the children and release the images to the media. Get them to sign a form saying they give you permission to release the photographs – it is best to cover your own back. You can never be too careful when it comes to children.

Events include trade shows, and you should be present at as many as possible that relate to your business or client, and sector. Take literature and information about your business or client and use the opportunity to meet and showcase yourself and them to interested individuals.

Guinness World Records

Many PR professionals have tapped into the potential PR advantages of breaking a world record. The process of setting a world record is free, unless you want an adjudicator present on the day. World record attempts are experiential and cohesive – they bring people together in pursuit of a single goal – and if well-thought-out can act as a great branding exercise.

Good world record attempts are tailored to the product or brand that is being promoted. For example, PR agency Frank PR set a world record for the largest audience for a video game performance, by inviting a journalist to use computer game DJ Hero, its client, at the Isle of Wight Festival. The upshot was a new world record and acres of coverage for the client, including a first-person piece from the journalist who had broken the record. The audience of 16,000 will have also felt engaged with both the record attempt and the product itself.

For PR purposes world record attempts involving the largest amount of people can be the most effective – for example, the largest amount of people dressed as Smurfs, or the largest amount of couples kissing (both genuine world records!). You are reaching an audience that is choosing to engage with you and will unite with you in a sense of achievement. The larger that audience the better!

A world record attempt is ambitious so do not undertake one lightly. The Guinness World Records website is your starting point if you fancy having a crack at it.

 brilliant definition

Stunts, events and activities form part of what is known as 'experiential marketing'. This helps consumers understand more about your brand, by interacting with it. Experiential activity can help bring consumers closer to you and your brand, by allowing them to touch, taste, see, smell or feel it, or interact with it in a range of sensory ways.

As the name suggests, experiential activity is all about giving consumers an experience. Furthermore consumers actively choose to participate in the activity, which is a more meaningful way of reaching and engaging with them than simply talking at them out of the pages of a newspaper or a TV advert.

The downsides of experiential activity are that it can be expensive, and the number of consumers you can reach with it are limited. You can get 100 or maybe 1,000 people to come to your event or experience, but 100,000 may read about you or your client in the media.

Experiential activity requires PR to succeed – people need to know what you are doing and how they can get involved. People also need to feel they are getting something out of the activity for themselves. They must learn something, receive something or achieve something to feel truly engaged.

Promotions and vouchers

Promotions can help generate interest in your business or client, and can also help you secure that elusive first-time customer. The rules of business state that it is generally easier to generate more business out of your existing customers than it is to find new ones, but at some point every business needs to grow.

Promotions could include:

- vouchers for discounts;
- loyalty card schemes such as the ones many coffee shops run whereby you stamp the card every time the customer makes a purchase and after a certain number of stamps the customer is entitled to a free product;
- clubcard schemes such as Nectar or Tesco Club Card where the customer is given 'points' that add up to deductions on their total bill after a period of time;
- arrangements with other businesses or companies to offer discounts on their products.

You can also use promotions to generate a message, for example, by including literature on product packaging. This technique has been used to great effect by cereal manufacturers who use the back of cereal packets, picked up by so many and scanned as they idly eat their breakfast, to house branded messages.

Running a promotion also allows you to ask customers for their contact details and helps you build up a database.

Charity events and CSR

Charity events can be a great way to do something worthy and benefit from the additional publicity it generates, but the event must be authentic. If people suspect you are running a charity event or fundraising initiative to raise your own or your client's profile first, and benefit the charity second, they will think twice before lending you their support.

Think about the size of charity your support can best benefit – smaller, locally based charities may be the right option for a small, locally based business. Alternatively, if you want to position yourself or your client as a business with a national or even global reach, aligning with a larger charity might be the best course of action.

You can add a charitable angle to your own event or activity, or run an event and activity purely to raise funds. Challenges are popular among the business community and make for good local newspaper stories – think local boss runs marathon or cycles for breast cancer.

Philanthropy, or corporate social responsibility (CSR) to give it its modern moniker, is a key plank of any successful business. If you are seen to be achieving, you must also be seen to be giving something back. The public expects businesses to act in a moral way, and it also expects businesses to contribute something back to the society which has helped make that business a success. For a small business, the CSR aspect only needs to be on a small scale, but supporting a local charity or organisation, such as a school or club, in an authentic, committed and genuine manner, can be worth its weight in gold.

CSR is about more than just charity however. It is about acting in a responsible way that can also help benefit your business or client. Switching to low-energy light bulbs, adopting a recycling policy, cutting down on waste or the amount of water and energy you consume, all count as CSR. You can also extend CSR strategy to actively participate in the local community, such as giving talks at local schools or business colleges, taking students on work experience, or organising mutually beneficial schemes for a network of local business, such as shared resources or a shared waste reduction scheme.

If you run your own business, in the early stages it may be tempting to overlook CSR, as it may have been tempting to overlook PR. But as your business grows, and comes under more intense scrutiny, you want to be seen to be doing the right thing. Most CSR initiatives also indirectly benefit the business, either by raising profile or cutting costs.

I would never advise a business to adopt a CSR strategy purely for the PR benefits, but suffice to say the PR benefits do come hand-in-hand with the CSR activity. A local paper may not, for example, cover your open day. But if your open day incorporates a raffle to raise funds for the local school, or a sponsored event that will raise money for charity, then the event moves beyond being simply a promotional activity into a genuine and newsworthy event of interest, and worthy of supporting. CSR can also help you with a news hook or USP – 'green business' is a more newsworthy topic than just 'business' and much more likely to be covered in the main pages of a publication, not just on the business pages.

Celebrities

Most celebrities are, to be honest, beyond the reach of a small business. Unless you happen to personally know a person of note or interest to the media, you are unlikely to be able to secure celebrity endorsement without a significant budget. There are also some celebrities who seemingly will lend their name to anything and these celebrities may be lower-budget but that is for a reason – celebrity endorsement, like charity endorsement, must seem authentic for it to be successful. A great example of this authenticity is Marco Pierre White's ongoing work with Knorr, which came about after the celebrity chef mentioned in an interview that Knorr stock cubes were his store cupboard staple. The firm promptly snapped him up to front their PR and advertising campaigns, and he does so in a manner that is believable and therefore effective.

If you do happen to know a celebrity or have a contact who does, then get them photographed at your business premises and a press release sent out about 'Our star visitor'. A celebrity, providing they can still legitimately be called that, is almost a sure-fire way into the press.

A more viable alternative for a smaller local business is to invite a local person of note to open your premises or speak at your event. Think local councillors, headteacher of the local school or your MP. The local press will generally want to cover something where a person of local interest is in attendance. By turn, councillors and MPs are usually pretty grateful for any publicity where they can be seen in a positive light as a pillar of the community supporting local enterprise.

Competitions

Running a competition is a great way to build up a customer database, one of the most valuable items you or your client will possess.

Simple techniques are often the most effective. Inviting customers to leave their business cards in a container for a monthly draw where the winner will receive a complimentary product or service is a technique adopted by many businesses. This costs nothing, allows the business to build a valuable database and get an idea of who is using their products or services, and the prize acts as an incentive.

You may also want to consider placing a competition in a newspaper or magazine. Most will happily run a competition as long as it ties in with the publication and its wider agenda. At the *Daily Echo* we ran a winter campaign one year called 'Beat the Freeze' aimed at helping the elderly stay warm on a budget (it is all glamour at daily papers!). For this, we were approached by several companies making, for example, thermal underwear, who wanted to associate themselves with the campaign by providing ten vests for us to give away.

A call to the features editor of the publication in question should be all that is needed. I can't speak for *Vogue*, but in general you should not be expected to pay to run a competition with a media outlet. Discuss with your contact at the publication whether you are going to provide the prizes up front, or whether they will send you names and addresses to forward the prizes to. The latter is preferable, it allows you to be prompt and add more names to your database. Also do not underestimate the busy journalist – sending out competition prizes can fall to the bottom of their 'to do' list.

Measuring and evaluating your campaign

PR professionals spend a huge amount of time measuring and evaluating the effectiveness of their activity. This is mainly because the true impact of PR is difficult to prove.

The industry wrestles with the dilemma of showing clients what their money has actually purchased – leading to odd measurements such as advertising value equivalent (AVE) which takes the size of the article in question and works out how much the client would have paid for an ad-slot that size. To pay homage to the fact that editorial coverage tends to be more trusted than paid-for coverage, this cost is then multiplied by three (or sometimes by ten) to provide a figure. This is why a great deal of PR campaigns will have ludicrous return on investments of £1 million for every £1 spent. Opportunity to see (OTS) is another measurement and basically counts the number of people who may have seen the article in question. However, this measurement is unscientific at best, as it relies on the circulation figures of that publication being accurate, and also on every single one of those readers having actively chosen to read the article in question from start to finish. Often multiple articles in one publication are counted separately, which can lead to OTS figures larger than the population of Great Britain.

As at this stage you are not paying a PR professional to do work for you, you probably do not need to be too concerned with OTS and AVE and other equally flawed measurements. If you are working for a client however they may expect to see AVE or OTS measurements and you should discuss their expectations at the beginning of your campaign.

It is always useful to evaluate the coverage you have received, so you can learn from the campaign. Look back at your original objectives. Have you moved closer to achieving them since the campaign began? For example, if you wanted to establish yourself as an industry spokesperson, have you gained coverage in trade and industry publications?

Look at traffic to your website. Were there any peaks or spikes, and if so, can you link this to a particular story or article that appeared about you or an activity run by you? Have you got more followers on Twitter or Facebook fans? Have you generated more traffic to your blog or noticed an increase in visitors to the blog?

Finally, look at sales. The ultimate aim of any PR campaign run by a business is to sell more. Have your sales increased since you began the campaign? Can you attribute any surges in orders or sales to a particular initiative, story or activity?

By understanding which coverage, activities and events have helped boost interest in you, traffic to your website and sales, you can work out what has been the most effective part of your campaign.

You need to know what works, PR wise, for your business or client to help with your ongoing PR strategy and future planning. If an article in a women's glossy magazine led to a flood of sales, then you now know that that magazine is a priority and you must work your hardest to keep a good relationship in the hope that they will feature you or your client again. Likewise, if an event was a success, make plans to repeat it. Your tried-and-tested formulas should not stop you trying something new, but if you know something works then, to coin a phrase, if it ain't broke, don't fix it!

 recap

- A PR campaign can give you a great boost and help generate more publicity for your business

- Events are a great way to engage with the public and experiential activity in general can get you closer to your customers and potential customers

- Involving a charity or some kind of CSR initiative in your campaigns is good for business and for PR purposes, but the effort must be believable

- Celebrity endorsement is expensive and ambitious, but involving local figures of note within your community can work well on a smaller scale

- Learn from your campaign so you know in future what works for you and what does not

CHAPTER 8

Crisis management

opefully you will never need to use the advice in this chapter, because you will never be on the receiving end of negative publicity, factual inaccuracies or overtly critical coverage. Unfortunately, journalists are entitled to express both facts and opinions and there is no law that says they have to be unrelentingly positive about you. Doubly unfortunately, journalists are human, like the rest of us, and sometimes make mistakes.

In the PR industry, crisis management (also called 'issues and crisis management' or 'firefighting') is something of an art, and there are individuals and entire agencies that exist purely to manage reputational crises, often crises of a national or even global scale. They are not always successful, but one peculiarity of this type of PR is that often success is judged by what is not published, as opposed to what is published. In essence, keeping a negative story to a minimum, or out of the media altogether, is a result in itself.

We do not need to concern ourselves with the finer points of the art of crisis management, as clearly any crisis befalling a small business or individual is hardly going to be of Deepwater Horizon-esque proportions. That said, for the small business owner or individual in question, such perspective may not be immediately available to them. Bad press can often feel like the end of the world.

 **tip**

The first and universal rule of crisis management is perspective. You are likely to feel emotional if you have your own business. It is your 'baby', your investment, your hard work, your blood, sweat and tears. For anyone to say or publish anything negative about it is equal to somebody insulting you personally.

Try and step back from your initial reaction, because quite often what you perceive as a hugely negative insult may be nothing more than a different way of phrasing something. If you find it impossible to be objective, ask a trusted friend or associate to give you their honest opinion of how negative or damaging the coverage is.

If possible, leave it 24 hours. This will give you time to digest and sleep on it, and to genuinely consider whether it is worth taking action. Avoid the temptation to pick up the phone and scream at the journalist in question. Even if they have wronged you in the worst way possible, this will not help you in the long run, because the second universal rule of crisis management is to remain calm and professional at all times.

If the bad press relates to the product or client you are representing, try to understand why they might feel emotional about it, and offer them an honest and objective opinion about the coverage.

There are four situations that may occur that would require some form of crisis management. They are:

- negative stories;
- factual inaccuracies;
- negative reviews;
- legal issues such as libel.

Once again though, it is very unlikely you will find your-self having to deal with all, if any, of these situations. Of the four potential crises, factual inaccuracies are by far the most common and very easily dealt with.

In all cases, you should expect to deal with the journalist who has written the story, even if they are a junior reporter, and not expect to be referred to someone senior or a line manager. Part of a journalist's job is to deal with complaints and errors. In some cases, your complaint may be dealt with by the features, news or section editor who takes responsibility for content pro-duced within their section.

It is very rare for editors and other very senior staff to deal with complaints unless they are extremely serious and involve legal issues.

Factual inaccuracies

If a factual inaccuracy has been printed or broadcast, then the media outlet is obliged to correct this. Online, it is much easier as the copy can be changed immediately. In the case of a newspaper, magazine or broadcast outlet, the correction must appear or occur in the next available edition. This is fine if the media outlet is daily, but a bit irritating if it is a weekly and downright maddening if it is a monthly!

The most common inaccuracies are mis-spelling names or cap-tioning pictures incorrectly. In the case of an incorrect caption, which usually occurs when there is more than one person in the photograph and the names are presented the wrong way round, most newspapers or magazines will without complaint publish a correction.

In the case of a mis-spelled name or company name, it is more likely that this will be put down to simple human error and not be corrected. Try and keep perspective when considering how hard you want to push for a correction. If your name is Claire and it has been spelled Clare, it is not really the end of the world. If your client's job title is CEO and they have appeared as MD, again, this is not the end of the world. If however your business's or client's name has been so dramatically mis-spelled that it has been given a different context or meaning, you have a case to argue.

The simplest course of action is to ring or email the journalist responsible and first and foremost thank them very much for the lovely piece they wrote, but unfortunately the following error has occurred and could it please be corrected in the next available edition? Follow up with an email with the correct spelling.

If you genuinely feel the factual inaccuracy could be detrimental to your business or client – for example, if the article says or implies it offers a product or service that it does not, then your best course of action is to explain to the journalist nicely why you feel what they have published is harmful to the business and ask if there is anything they can do to correct this, whether this be publish a correction or run a follow-up article clarifying the situation. An implication is not a fact, so you cannot demand a correction, but you can ask for one and explain why you think it is justified.

Do bear in mind however that it is not the job of a journalist to promote or plug your business or client. Their job is to inform and entertain their readers – the two are not always compatible. Wherever possible, emphasise that readers will want to know the correct facts, not that your business or client might suffer.

Negative stories

Legally speaking, if a media outlet intends to publish something factually negative about your business or client, it is obliged to contact you or the client for a comment and to offer you the chance to respond.

The emphasis here is of course on 'factually' negative. By factually negative I mean a story that will make a claim about you or your business that the journalist believes to be true and can prove through their sources.

For a small business, the most likely negative press would be a disgruntled customer feeling they have been badly treated and taking their case to the press. In this case, the media outlet must try to make contact with you to offer you the chance to comment.

 example

Imagine a customer has rung a newsdesk and complained that they feel they have not been treated well by you – they placed an order and it has not arrived in a reasonable period of time, a staff member was rude to them, they were breastfeeding on your premises and asked to stop, or the quality of the product or service was not in keeping with what they were originally promised.

What should happen

The journalist who has been given the story should telephone or email you explaining the nature of the complaint and inviting your response.

What to do

Make sure you are 100 per cent clear on the nature of the complaint. Ask the journalist to explain it to you thoroughly and follow up with an email outlining the complaint, if possible a copy of the complaint if it is in written form. Ask for any other evidence the journalist has, such as a photograph or some other way they can prove their claim. Ask for the name of the complainant so you can check it against records, but be aware that the journalist might not be prepared to let you have the name if they feel it would harm their source. Finally, ask the journalist what deadline they are working to and say you will get back to them with a response within this timeframe, and take as many contact details for that journalist as possible – email address, phone number and mobile – to ensure you can get hold of them in time. ▶

What next

Investigate the complaint thoroughly so you are absolutely clear of what has happened at your end – ask any members of staff to explain the situation if it did not involve you personally, and check all paperwork relating to the complaint if you have any. From this, you can formulate your response, in consultation with your client if necessary. Ideally, this will be to offer the customer a full refund, unless we are talking very large sums of money, in which case at least try and offer them a discount. You may also want to consider offering the customer a discount on future purchases, a complimentary experience or product, or a face-to-face meeting with you or the client to discuss their concerns and come up with a resolution. If the complaint relates to health and safety or hygiene, consider whether it is a genuine one-off fluke, or if you or the client require further training in this area.

Your response

It is tempting simply to offer no comment, in the hope that the story will 'go away'. Unless there are very mitigating circumstances, it will not. You are free to use any relationship you have with the journalist in question to try and persuade them to 'go easy' on you, but bear in mind no matter how nice a journalist has been to you in the past, if they feel the story is a good one, they will run it no matter how much they like you. Pleas are likely to fall on deaf ears. They will probably also have discussed the story with their news editor or other senior staff member in a news meeting, so the decision whether or not to run the story will have been taken out of their hands.

It is best to provide a response via email, as this reduces the risk of being misquoted and provides you with a paper trail. So if you feel you are unfairly represented in the final write-up, you have a copy of your statement to hand to which you can refer.

Your response should contain:

- the date, time and particulars of the incident and who was involved;
- what happened, as factually as possible (try and avoid apportioning blame either to yourself or to the complainant unless it is utterly justified);

- what the resolution is (the action you have decided to take – offering the customer a full apology and refund, and any further action you will be taking such as further training in this area or a review of suppliers);

- a quote from yourself or the client, expressing your feelings on the matter in a clear and concise way: 'We are sorry for any inconvenience caused to Mr Bloggs and hope the matter is now resolved to his satisfaction. Should he have any further queries, we will treat the matter as a priority.' You may also want to put in a 'key message' style quote such as 'Customer service is crucially important to us and we value all feedback', but do not be surprised if this does not get used.

Pitfalls

Do not issue a flat-out denial in the hope the story will go away. If there genuinely is no truth whatsoever in the claim or complaint, then respond accordingly, but make sure you can back this up. A flat denial without any way of backing this up will simply make the journalist work harder to prove that the complaint or allegation against you is true.

If you promise something, deliver it. For example, if your response is to offer the customer their money back, do it. If you say you or your client is going to take a product off the shelves, make sure you do so immediately. Do not be surprised if the journalist checks up on you!

It is good practice however to deal with every complaint or criticism you receive before the individual starts phoning up the papers.

Negative reviews

Under normal circumstances, if a media outlet publishes something negative, critical and detrimental about you, this could be libel (see Legal issues, below). One exception however is if the person is expressing an opinion, usually within a review.

If the opinion is honestly held and published without malice (the person does not have a massive vendetta against you), then that individual is entitled to their opinion. Most reviewers do strive to be balanced and fair. Your offering may not be their cup of tea, but they will in most cases recognise that it will appeal to some. A truly dreadful, appalling review is rare. You will need to have done something very wrong to be on the receiving end of a complete trashing.

brilliant dos and don'ts

✔ DO remember the golden rule and try and keep your perspective. Has the reviewer been fair? Have they identified that, whilst this was not for them, there are people who would enjoy or appreciate it? Have they picked out positives as well as negatives? Have they said why they were so unimpressed and is any of it ringing true? For example, if you run a high-end restaurant and they have said there was too much 'jus' and 'confit' and not enough good old-fashioned grub for their liking, that is their opinion and they are entitled to it. Fans of jus and confit – your ideal customers – will not be deterred.

✘ DON'T ask for an apology or a correction unless the review contains a factual inaccuracy.

✔ DO bear in mind that the general public knows that a review is only the opinion of one person.

✘ DON'T dwell on the review. If you can learn from it, then do so, but otherwise try and put it behind you and concentrate on generating more, better reviews from other sources.

✔ DO keep up your relationship with the media outlet that has run the review. The reviewer may not necessarily be the journalist you are used to dealing with, so do not hold it against them.

Legal issues

I cannot emphasise enough how unlikely it is that you will ever need to become involved in taking legal action against a media outlet. In my eight years as a journalist, I have never even come close to being threatened with legal action – and I have certainly had my fair share of complaints, angry phonecalls and even a particularly abusive man coming into reception and threatening to 'get' me.

Despite this, it is worth having a basic grasp of libel law. Libel is really the only possible legal scenario you could find yourself in but once again, it is hugely unlikely. So treat this section as 'useful to know' rather than 'need to know'.

 brilliant   definition

Libel

Libel and the spoken equivalent, slander, refers to the publication or broadcast of an untrue or false statement that:

- exposes someone to hatred, ridicule or contempt; or
- causes them to be shunned or avoided; or
- disparages them in their office, profession or trade; or
- lowers them in the estimation of right-thinking members of society.

The crucial element here is that the libellous statement must be false. If you have been convicted of fraud and a newspaper calls you a 'fraudster', you cannot sue for libel, because the statement is true.

Libel can be caused by an unchecked fact that reflects badly on you, or by an innuendo or implication. Libel can also occur completely by accident, if a journalist publishes a statement that, even indirectly, causes any of the above – exposure to hatred and so on.

What journalists are taught about libel

Newspapers are terrified of libel and rightly so, not only because it is exceptionally bad practice to publish untruths, but also because libel cases are difficult to defend and can result in the newspaper having to pay vast sums of money to the wronged party, plus all their legal costs.

Journalists are taught to:

- check and preferably double-check all their facts;
- always approach the person or organisation they are at risk of libelling to allow them to give their side of the story – this is known as 'right of reply' and it is a *right*;
- be specific and make it clear exactly who they are referring to when publishing anything negative, such as a court case. Local newspapers in particular are scrupulous about identifying defendants. 'John Smith of Woodvale has been convicted of murder' is not acceptable, as there may be many John Smiths living in Woodvale. 'John Smith, 41, of Acacia Avenue, Woodvale has been convicted of murder' avoids the risk of every John Smith in the village suing the newspaper for implying they are a murderer.

A journalist should only publish a negative story that is potentially libellous if they know and can prove beyond all reasonable doubt that the story is true.

When it comes to libel cases, the burden of proof rests with the defendant. This means that the defendant – the media outlet – must be able to prove their story is true. The claimant does not have to *prove* the story is false. This puts the pressure even more on the media to get their facts right – and rightly so.

What to do if you think you or your client has been libelled

Consult a lawyer as soon as possible. It is essential you take legal advice as libel can be excruciatingly expensive. If the lawyer thinks you have a case, then you can press charges.

Most libel cases are settled out of court. This is because the media outlet, knowing the horrendous cost and difficulty of defending libel, will consider it to be less costly in the long run to offer the claimant a substantial sum of money (usually reported as 'undisclosed damages') and a full apology. There is no cap on the amount of damages a court can order a media outlet guilty of libel to pay the claimant, which is one of the many reasons that England is currently the libel capital of the world.

Many feel English libel law is outdated, and that its emphasis on payment of damages over the strength of an apology makes libel more about financial gain than protecting reputation.

Turning a negative story into a positive one

As mentioned at the beginning of this chapter, there are PR teams and agencies devoted to crisis management. Part of this remit is turning negative stories into positive, or at the very least neutral, coverage.

 example

BBC 6 Music

In early 2010, the BBC announced its intention to close its digital radio station 6 Music as part of a 'strategic review', or money-saving drive in layman's terms. The announcement was greeted with outrage by the music community and a series of high-profile celebrities and bands including Coldplay, Lily Allen, David Bowie and Jarvis Cocker spoke out in defence of the station. The broadcaster received more than 2,500 complaints from

▶

members of the public about the plans. An online campaign, which had been sparked in late 2009 when rumours of plans to axe the station first surfaced, netted the support of more than 70,000 people on Facebook alone.

The BBC Trust subsequently rejected the plans to close 6 Music, noting that listener figures had risen from 600,000 at the time of the review, to one million following the announcement that the station was to close.

The entire saga was such a spectacular success for the BBC that some have even suggested it never intended to close 6 Music in the first place but simply wanted to round up public support and increase audience figures for the struggling station. Whether the story as it unfolded was genuine, or an elaborate PR campaign, one thing is for sure, the BBC came out of the whole thing smelling of the sweetest of roses. It went from people's villain to hero of the people, 'saving' its own station, and providing a substantial boost to listener figures in the process, no doubt inspired by the many credible, heavyweight celebrities the campaign ensnared.

 **brilliant** recap

- Negative press is rare so do not spend too much time worrying about it
- If someone has printed or broadcast something factually inaccurate you can ask for this to be corrected in the next available edition or programme
- Reviews are based upon the opinion of one person and reviewers are entitled to give their honest opinions of your product or service, even if it is not what you would like them to say
- Keep your perspective when dealing with any inaccuracies or negative press
- There is always the potential to turn a negative into a positive

CHAPTER 9

The next steps

rilliant PR has so far looked at the basic skills involved in creating a PR strategy for your business, or for any product or client you are promoting. We have looked at identifying and creating a brand and USP, media relations, pitching, online presence, social media and networking, and looked at how to plan a campaign. We have also dipped our toes into crisis management, a particular PR skill that hopefully you will never need to use, and examined some very basic media law.

If you have gone ahead and put the key areas into action, you may, by this stage, have some experience of dealing with the media and have built some relationships with a few key journalists. You may also have an eye on your target media and be regularly reading, watching or listening to it and keeping up to date with developments. Your Facebook page and Twitter feed may have attracted fans and followers and your blog may be being read, if only by a few key individuals, and may even be generating comments and questions from readers. So, what next?

Maintaining and reviewing your strategy

News is constantly evolving – and as we have already discussed, the media, particularly the digital media, are also constantly evolving. This means your PR strategy must be flexible and adaptable. Journalists change jobs, media are overhauled, relaunched and sometimes closed down. Your customers are constantly evolving too. New products, new technology, new ways of working and new trends all constantly shape and influence what your customers demand.

One trend that shows no sign of going away is an increased desire from customers for transparency and openness from the brands and businesses they choose to interact with. This is one of the many reasons why a PR strategy is essential in the first place. Customers want to know more and more about the products and services they consume. Where do these products and services come from? Who makes them? What are they made of? Are they ethical? Organic? Fairtrade? Sustainable? Recyclable? Does the company have a CSR strategy and is it seen to act in an ethical and appropriate way? Is that company seen to be active in its local and business communities?

brilliant tip

Your PR strategy must be constantly addressing this desire from customers for transparency. Take a look at the list below. How many of the following are you doing on a daily, weekly or monthly basis?

- Updating your website.
- Writing your blog.
- Updating your Facebook page.
- Tweeting.
- Sending out newsletters to customers.
- Sending press releases to the media.
- Building relationships with journalists.
- Responding to media inquiries and queries from members of the public.
- Hosting and attending events, workshops and open days.

- Working to help the local community through fundraising and other activities.
- Reviewing and updating your customer database.
- Reviewing and updating your media database.
- Networking and building contacts within the local and business communities.
- Sharing and exchanging knowledge relevant to your sector.

It sounds like a lot of effort, but these activities will all help you remain visible and accountable. Remember the first chapter and introduction to this book? How can people purchase your products or services, if they do not know you are there? People forget very, very quickly.

As your business or client progresses and grows, it is more important than ever to press ahead with your PR strategy. Review it from time to time. Which media outlets are you currently targeting and which could you be targeting? How could you improve your website, blog or Facebook page? How can you get more Twitter followers? How could you encourage more customers to find out about your business or client? How can you help the community and your own business or client at the same time?

Overkill

As much as I have emphasised the importance of building relationships with journalists and keeping yourself and your business visible, there is such a thing as overkill. I have worked at several publications where we have imposed a 'ban' on an individual or company for a few weeks or months, as it got to the point where that individual or company was in the publication every single week.

Likewise as a journalist I have been put off by PR contacts who persist in bombarding me with pointless 'news stories' that are of no interest to anybody but them, along with regular chirpy phonecalls along the lines of 'just seeing what you've got coming up and if we can get involved'.

I would class both of these occurrences as lazy. The first is lazy on the part of the media outlet, for not finding a broad enough range of stories or people and instead falling back on the same old contacts time and time again. The second is lazy on the part of the PR professional, for hoping a scattergun approach will lead to success (it will not) and for not taking the time to prepare suggestions and ideas for stories and features, instead of just ringing up and asking what they can get involved in.

Avoiding overkill is relatively simple. Ask yourself, before you pick up the phone or press 'send', if what you are doing is going to be of use to the journalist. Are they really going to run a press release about the fact that you have appointed a PA? Unless you are Sir Alan Sugar, then I would say no. Use your judgement, which will become more attuned to the news agenda the more you work at it. Have you ever read a story in your target publication that is similar to the story you are pitching in? If not, think carefully and ask yourself – is this something I would want to read, if it were not about me or my business?

Your priority is to remain useful. Rather than phoning 'to see what you've got coming up', put together a few ideas and send them by email, along with an invitation to lunch to see if any of the ideas might work for that journalist. Remember the golden rules we discussed in the media relations and pitching chapters. If you find yourself tempted to break any of them, stop, think – and don't!

Wider marketing

PR can only do so much. The new buzzword is 'integrated marketing' – combining PR with advertising, direct marketing, experiential marketing, digital activity and wider marketing initiatives. There are advantages and disadvantages to all marketing disciplines. Advertising is a guaranteed 'hit' – you pay, you get an advert, people see or hear it. Direct marketing allows you to target people individually. PR gets you editorial coverage and public exposure. Experiential marketing allows to you interact with customers, and digital activity helps you engage with them and start conversations.

When you reach the stage where you feel your business or client needs, or is ready for, a real 'push', I strongly recommend talking to other businesses about their wider marketing strategies, and marketing and advertising professionals, who will help you find the right strategy for your business. You will need to set aside a budget, as PR is the only marketing discipline that can be done at more or less no cost to you other than your own time.

Taking on PR support

If you run your own business, at some point, you will become so busy with work that is essential to your business – be that generating new business, client/customer relations or production – that you may simply not have the time to continue with your PR strategy.

This is an inevitable and very welcome consequence of the growth of your business. Even with the best will in the world, once you reach that happy time when your business is becoming so successful that you are simply rushed off your feet, it is so easy to let things slide. That press release remains unwritten, you never quite get round to taking that photo and sending it in to the local paper, you would really like to do another open day but you do not have the time to organise it, and that blogpost you meant to put up two weeks ago is still all in your head, not on your computer, spelling and grammar-checked.

And let's be honest here, PR is not the kind of business tool that can yield you an immediate, financial result. The process of building and managing a reputation can be long, slow and tiresome, and the full results may not be immediately apparent. This further adds to the temptation to just put your PR on hold for a while. You will start again when you have more time.

As a person who has been motivated enough to plan and set up their own business and run a basic PR strategy, you will know full well you will never 'have' more time. You may even be at the stage where you are unable to make more time. This is when you may want to consider taking on some kind of PR help or support.

PR training

If you own a business, one option is to undergo formal PR training yourself, or have a member of staff trained up to take on the PR for your business. If you are representing a client or product, you may suggest members of the client's team are trained up in PR to save you time. This does not need to be a full-time member of staff, and the PR focus does not need to be full time either. So if you or the client has a part-time PA who comes in twice a week, you could think about having them trained to take on some of the PR duties, either within their current hours or adding to their weekly hours.

You may want to try and train them up yourself, using the skills and techniques you have learned through this book, or have a PR or similar professional run some workshops or training for them.

Finding training

Freelance PR consultants and small start-up agencies often offer training, as do PR agencies, although the latter are likely to charge more for their expertise. The best way to find a decent trainer is to simply ask around – whether that is asking local PR agencies or other small businesses that have had PR training. Some freelance journalists will also offer PR and media relations training.

As is so often the case however, asking other small businesses in your area how they have approached PR training might lead to the best, and most cost-effective, option for you.

What to train staff in

The strengths and weaknesses of staff are likely to determine what, if any, aspects of PR you want them trained in. You should be able to find training on:

- identifying news hooks and angles;
- writing press releases;
- media relations and pitching;
- crisis management;
- social media.

Alternatively you may want to send staff to group sessions or workshops, or arrange a PR training session with other small businesses in your area to share the cost.

Avoid giving PR duties to staff members who are uncomfortable or nervous talking on the phone. As you know yourself by now, PR involves a lot of time talking to journalists, answering questions and finding information. It helps in these circumstances to have a degree of confidence talking on the phone, and to not be prone to panicking if put on the spot or asked questions.

Taking on freelance PR support

Whether or not you have a staff member trained in PR, if you would like to run a targeted PR campaign or really push a particular project, freelance support can be a cost-effective solution.

Freelance PR professionals may have worked for brands, organisations or agencies in PR roles and chosen to pursue a freelance lifestyle instead, or they may be former journalists or also work as freelance journalists and use PR as a way to top up their income. Whichever route they have taken, they are likely to have a broad knowledge of PR and be competent and capable. You can find freelance PR professionals through networks such as LinkedIn, but as with anything word of mouth is the best way forward, so again, ask around.

The advantages of using a freelancer include:

- Flexibility – they can work to your requirements and work by the hour or by the day.
- Cost-effectiveness – freelancers have lower overheads and therefore can offer more competitive rates than a full-blown PR agency.
- Contacts – freelancers should have a good range of contacts from previous work they have undertaken.

Good freelancers are not always instantly available – they may be booked up for months in advance – and this is a testimony to their ability. If you choose to use freelance PR support, it is worth taking the time to find the right person and developing an ongoing relationship with them.

You can employ a freelancer on a project-by-project basis, or you can negotiate for someone to come in on a regular basis to take care of your PR. Freelance PR professionals should have excellent writing skills and be able to update your website copy, and also have a good grasp of social media so you may want to hand over your Twitter feed and Facebook page to them too. Make sure you trust the quality of their work before you give them all your passwords. If you feel the need to try out a few freelancers before sticking with one, do so. A good relationship is worth taking the time to build.

Taking on a PR agency

There are many advantages to taking on a PR agency. You can use their contacts and creativity, and a good agency should be able to suggest numerous clever and creative campaigns to boost your public profile. An ongoing relationship with an agency means it can get to know your business inside out and become part of its development, helping point you in the direction of future ideas and business initiatives that will help you grow and improve as well as generate a buzz.

In general, as with most things, you will get what you pay for. That does not mean you should brace yourself to fork out thousands a month for a big-name agency. Rather that if a PR agency appears to be quoting you dramatically competitive rates but promising the earth, you would do well to be sceptical.

You can take on an agency on a retained basis, meaning that they will spend a certain amount of time a month working for you in return for an agreed monthly fee. Alternatively, you can take agencies on a project-by-project basis, paying them only to work on specific projects or campaigns.

How to find a PR agency

In some cases, agencies may actively contact you, especially if you have been making an effort with your own PR. Some agencies scout for new business by paying close attention to businesses and organisations that appear in the media, and simply phoning them up and asking if they are interested in any PR support. It is always worth considering an agency that has taken the time and effort to approach you, but do not feel you have to take them on or allow yourself to be pressured into anything.

There are services that can help match clients with PR agencies – for example, the Public Relations Consultants Association runs a service that is free to the client and searches through members to find six agencies that match what you are looking for. This can save you a lot of work, but the association will only recommend agencies that are members of the PRCA, and many smaller, more regionally based agencies are not.

Read trade press, such as the venerable *PRWeek*, and look at which agencies have been winning awards. For the purposes of a smaller business the CIPR PRide Awards, which are regional awards that take place every year between October and Christmas, are a good way of seeing which local and regional agencies are doing well. Awards are not everything, but they are a good indication of an agency that is performing well. Every year *PRWeek* publishes the Top 150, a list of the 150 highest-earning agencies in the industry that give us their financial information. This does not include all high-earning agencies as some decline to give their figures, but those that do provide useful information including how much they made in fees, number of clients and number of staff. The Top 150 also shows which agencies are growing.

Word of mouth is the best way to find a good PR agency. Ideally, you want an agency that has similar clients to yourself. It is certainly impressive if a PR agency can boast Coca Cola or Nike as a client but as a small business you will have very different needs to large, global brands (and very different budgets!). However some clients specify that their agency may not work with direct competitors so if an agency works for a direct rival, they might not also be able to work for you.

Types of PR agency

There is a huge range of PR agencies out there including:

- *Networks*: Large marcomms groups such as WPP own several PR agencies, as well as advertising, digital and marketing agencies. Agencies operate as individual companies with their own management, and have offices globally as well as in the UK. Networks have excellent contacts and people, train staff to a high level in-house and often have global reach. They can however be expensive and focused on big-money accounts.

- *Independent agencies*: The majority of PR agencies are independent, meaning they are separate businesses. They sometimes work alongside other independent agencies in other countries or have offices in other countries, depending on the size of the agency. They also sometimes work alongside advertising or digital agencies on integrated projects. Independent agencies vary hugely in size, scope and quality and it is impossible to attribute many characteristics to them as a group.

- *Generalist agencies*: PR agencies may specialise or they may be 'generalist' in that they will take on and work across all sectors. Generalist agencies tend to be larger and operate in teams such as a consumer team, healthcare team, etc.

- *Specialist agencies*: There are many specialisms within PR and many agencies devoted to these specialist sectors. Specialist agencies could cover consumer PR, entertainment and showbiz, healthcare PR, technology, digital, public sector, voluntary sector, lobbying and public affairs. They could also cover a particular media, such as broadcast, or a particular demographic, such as young people or older people or a region. There are also PR agencies that specialise in small businesses and entrepreneurs.

Appointing an agency

Whether you have approached an agency or individual to do your PR or they have approached you, take your time over the process and talk to a range of agencies and individuals. The standard procedure is for clients to invite agencies to submit expressions of interest. The client then holds a pitch which can include the following stages:

- Agencies presenting information about themselves, their work and their current clients (where appropriate) to help the client put together a shortlist.

- Agencies responding to a particular brief from the client and presenting how they would approach the client's individual requirements, whether that is long-term support or an individual project or campaign.

- 'Chemistry meetings' where the client and agency brainstorm ideas and suggestions about how best to work together.

Pitching is time-consuming and expensive for the client and the agency. There are some within the PR industry who believe that pitching is a flawed process that should not exist. You can understand why – no agency wants to spend time and effort putting together great ideas for a client only to see the work go to someone else or worse, the client simply use their ideas to inform their own future campaigns. For this reason agencies will evaluate at the start whether the rewards on offer are worth the time and effort spent trying to get the business.

At this stage it is probably better to enter into conversations, informally at first, with PR agencies and freelancers to find out what they can offer you, and to get an idea of how much you need to be prepared to pay. You can also discuss how you will measure the success of their work for you.

Whoever you appoint, make sure you are 100 per cent happy and remain 100 per cent happy. PR is a service industry and keeping the client happy is front and centre. If you feel you are not getting value for money or not receiving what you have been led to believe, then treat your PR agency as you would any other supplier. Discuss your concerns, agree a way forward and, if necessary, seek an alternative agency.

A good agency should:

- take your calls or return ther
- keep you regularly updateu you;
- get to know you and your business;
- demonstrate knowledge and awareness of your ᴄ your wider sector;
- have fresh ideas and suggestions for future campaigns;
- listen to any concerns and act upon them;
- not promise the earth – by this stage you know very well that there are few guarantees in PR. Some agencies operate on a guaranteed return on investment model, drawing up a plan of exactly what they will set out to achieve for the client. This is useful in terms of evaluation, but an agency promising you 100 media hits in one month is going to employ any means necessary to get you into anything that could be construed as 'media'. If given this option or the option of an agency that will work hard to get you a few, very valuable media hits in top-tier publications, go with the latter. Quality is always better than quantity.

However you choose to move forward, your PR strategy remains one of the most vital weapons at your disposal. Reputation is precious and customers want to trust the businesses they choose to associate with and more importantly, spend money with. There is no substitute for a good reputation and the best way to build one is through consistent, well-planned and thoughtful PR. A good PR strategy, whether you choose to keep on managing it yourself or outsource it, is simply good business sense.

recap

Keep up with your PR strategy – out of sight really does mean out of mind

- Choose your PR support carefully and treat a PR agency or consultant as you would any other supplier

- Talk to other businesses about their PR strategy and take recommendations from people you trust about PR agencies and consultants

- Good PR makes good business sense

Conclusion

When I was researching this book, I met with a friend and most exemplary businesswoman, Catherine Birch. Catherine is an interior designer and runs Silver Birch Designs.

We discussed the concept of the book over lunch. Catherine was as interested in grilling me about PR as I was in asking her all about life as a successful business owner. We both agreed that a book like this, helping people like her to understand and master PR, was generally a pretty good idea.

I asked her about generating business opportunities and keeping herself in the public eye and she said something that I consider vital to the overall theme of this book. She told me that a lot of her time is spent telephoning clients, former clients and potential clients. She asks them how they are, discusses business, takes them out for lunch where needed. Because, she said, it is so easy for people to forget you. You might have done the most brilliant job known to man, but if it was six months ago people will already start to forget. To stay at the top of someone's mind you have to be visible. People have to know you are there, still in business, still interested in their custom and still interested in them.

Your PR strategy is those phonecalls and lunches. It is about staying visible. There are so many businesses and enterprises in the UK, so how can anybody be expected to remember all but the very biggest, whose branding is everywhere and who are constantly beaming messages out of the TV and radio and in your line of vision every time you open a newspaper.

Using PR will help your business or client get ahead and stay ahead. Ignore it at your peril. But equally, enjoy it. Despite all the warnings in this book, especially about media relations, PR is fun. That is the reason so many people want to work within the industry. PR involves dealing with fun, nice people and planning great events and campaigns that everybody will enjoy. It is a happy, positive industry most of the time. And PR is a happy, positive practice most of the time, so do not think of it as a chore. Yes, at times it is hard work and sometimes it is not immediately rewarding, but the journey should be, overall, a positive one.

Good luck!

Index

the brilliant series